A Cowboy in the Kitchen

A Cowboy in the Kitchen

Recipes from Reata and Texas West of the Pecos

GRADY SPEARS

AND ROBB WALSH

Food photography by Dick Patrick
Location photography by James Evans

Ten Speed Press
Berkeley, California

To my grandfather, W.W. Spears

1⊜

Ten Speed Press
P.O. Box 7123
Berkeley, California 94707
www.tenspeed.com

Distributed in Australia by Simon and Schuster Australia, in Canada by Ten Speed Press Canada, in New Zealand by Southern Publishers Group, in South Africa by Real Books, in Southeast Asia by Berkeley Books, and in the United Kingdom and Europe by Airlift Book Company.

Cover and interior design by Catherine Jacobes
Food photography by Dick Patrick
Food styling by Brooke Leonard
Location photography by James Evans

We would like to thank the following firms for their assistance with props for the food photography:

Pris Hodges and Jill O'Connor at Prairie Rose
3404 Camp Bowie, Ft. Worth, TX 76107, (817) 332-4369 or (888) 776-7357

El Paso Import Co.
4524 McKinney Avenue, Suite 102, Dallas, TX 75205, (214) 559-0907

Library of Congress Cataloging-in-Publication Data

Spears, Grady.
   A cowboy in the kitchen: recipes from West Texas's Reata Restaurant / Grady Spears and Robb Walsh.
      p. cm.
   ISBN 1-58008-004-9
   1. Cookery, American—Western style. 2. Cowboys—Texas, West. 3. Reata Restaurant. I. Walsh, Robb. II. Title
TX715.2.W47S65   1998
641.5978—dc21   98-8210
                                    CIP

First printing, 1998
Printed in Hong Kong

6 7 8 9 10 — 05 04 03 02

Contents

Contents

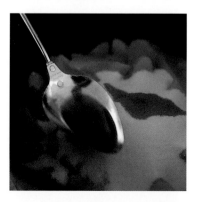

Grady Spears, Al Micallef, and Mike Evans
of the Reata Restaurant group.

Acknowledgments

The authors would like to thank Cliff Teinert for the historical background. Brad Whitfield for the sourdough baking tips. Bobby McKnight, Joaquin Jackson, William "Billito" Donnell and Joe Richardson for their wild stories. Thanks also to the talented food professionals who helped shape these recipes: Kris Ackerman, Brooke Leonard, Louis Lambert, Brian Olenjack, Reggie Ferguson, Lupe Sanchez, Robert Hicks, Mark Rose, Todd Phillips, Juan Jarmillo, Tim Love, Fred Hamilton, Nacho, and all the staff at Reata Restaurants — without you guys this book wouldn't have happened! And to Dick Patrick and his staff.

The Reata Group would like to thank K.C. Sorber for his tireless dedication, and the best group of managers anyone could ever have: Reggie Parks, Kyle Moch, Grant Kernan, Wade Sanders, Marcus Graves, and Kirk Kampfhenkel, who keep everything running! Also many thanks to all the other people who have contributed to Reata's success: Mike and Alice Stevens; Richard Burns; Carla Curry; Billy Williams; Kim Rotan; Tommy Johns; the guys at Ben E. Keith, Doug, Steve, Del, and Jan; Big Bend Saddlery; and the girls at Prairie Rose, Priss and Jill!

Grady wishes to thank Sara for putting up with all of his adventures; and his parents and parents-in-law for all the support. Hats off to Denny Hayes, who believed in the project from the start. Last but not least to all the people of Alpine, Fort Worth, and the great state of Texas for supporting the cowboy culture. Happy Trails!

Preface

Reata means "rope" in Spanish, but in Texan mythology the word means a lot more. Reata was the name of the ranch in *Giant,* a book by Edna Ferber that was made into an movie in 1956. The film starred Elizabeth Taylor and James Dean and won nine Academy Awards. In the book and the movie, the Reata Ranch and the cattle culture of the Old West struggle to survive in the brash new economic reality brought on by the discovery of oil.

The tension between the cultures of the Old West and the New West explored in *Giant* may seem like old hat to the rest of the world by now, but in Texas the theme has a stubborn timeliness. Though most Texans may be far removed from the state's ranching heritage and totally subsumed in the electronic global village these days, the cowboy culture remains a touchstone for Texans, continuing to influence the way we think, the way we act, the way we dress, and the way we eat.

Nowhere is our cowboy legacy more carefully preserved or highly regarded than in the Trans-Pecos region. Thanks both to the absence of oil and an environment uniquely suited to large-scale ranching, the Trans-Pecos remains the last preserve of the old-time Texas cattle culture. On the ranches of the Trans-Pecos, things are still done the old-fashioned way, if only to keep the old way alive. Western artwork, saddle making and leather crafts, cowboy poetry, cowboy cooking, and all the other forms of creative expression the Old West gave us continue to thrive in the Trans-Pecos. The Trans-Pecos still looks and feels like the Old West, which is why decades of Westerns, including *Giant,* were filmed there.

When we decided to open our first restaurant in Alpine, we wanted it to play a part in preserving Western culture. The restaurant serves what we call West Texas cowboy cuisine. It's decorated with the brand of my ranch, the CF, the brands of neighboring ranches, and a collection of authentic Western artifacts.

When it came time to name the restaurant, we decided to call it Reata, after the mythical ranch in *Giant* and the cattle culture it represented.

—AL MICALLEF, CF Ranch
Co-Owner, Reata Restaurants

Introduction

BACK WHEN I WAS PUNCHING COWS, if you'd told me I was going to be a chef someday, I would have doubled up in laughter and fallen off my horse. To tell the truth, I still feel a little funny about calling myself a chef. At the Reata restaurants, we've got guys in the kitchen who've spent years in cooking schools earning their white hats. These guys know French cooking inside out. Me, when I hear somebody say they're getting out the mandolin, I still expect to hear some country-and-western tunes.

It's only a couple of miles from the stockyards where I used to work as a cowboy to the Reata Restaurant in downtown Fort Worth where I am the head chef, but let me tell you, that couple of miles was a long strange trip.

I never thought I'd ever be anything but a cowboy. When I was fourteen, my family lived in Granbury, just outside of Fort Worth. I was always hanging around friends' ranches, riding horses and helping with the cattle. I even joined the Future Farmers of America chapter at my high school. One time, the club went to a livestock show in Houston, and I got into the calf scramble.

In a calf scramble, they let ten calves loose and twenty kids run around trying to catch them. If you catch a calf, you get to keep it. Well, I ran around the Astrodome

like an idiot, chasing calves until I finally got one. It was red and white and weighed 180 pounds. I was ecstatic, despite the fact that my family lived in a subdivision and there was no way my mama was going to let me raise livestock in the backyard. I talked one of my friends into letting me keep my calf on his ranch.

That calf was my pride and joy. I was going to raise it and win first place at the livestock show. When my folks announced that we were moving into the city of Fort Worth that year, I was so upset about losing my calf that they let me stay in Granbury at my friend's ranch until my freshman year was over.

You'd think that moving to the city would have ended my cowboy fantasies, but I just got all the more determined. In my new high school in Fort Worth, I applied for the vocational training program and got a job in the stockyards. I got out of school early a couple of days a week to go down to the Vann-Roach cattle brokerage and chase cattle around. It was dirty work—branding, inoculating, castrating—and the Fort Worth stockyards weren't exactly the open range, but I figured I was way ahead of everybody else because this was my life's dream.

I got an agriculture scholarship, but I hated college. I quit after six weeks and went to work full-time at Vann-Roach. They made me a cattle buyer, which sounded great at the time. I was nineteen years old, and I was going to livestock auctions all over the state bidding against the old timers. I guess those old-timers got the best of me. I was paid on commission, and I didn't earn diddly-squat. In fact, I was starving. I remember going a whole week eating nothing but cereal.

I started looking for a second job to make ends meet. A restaurant called Epicure on the Park hired me as a bus boy. It was my first job in the restaurant business and the main reason I took it was because I thought I might get some free food along with the paycheck.

After a while, somebody quit, and they asked me if I wanted to be a waiter. I made a lot more money waiting tables than I ever did as a cowboy, so eventually I quit my job at Vann-Roach. Then I took a job in Houston managing a restaurant called Moveable Feast. It was a strange time for me since I still thought of myself as a cattleman, and here I was running a vegetarian restaurant. That's when I met J. P. Bryan, the owner of the Gage Hotel in Marathon. Bryan was looking for somebody to manage the restaurant at his hotel.

When you cross the Pecos River, you enter a time warp, a place where the traditions of the Old West are still alive.

I had never been to Marathon, so I went down to check it out. The restaurant at the Gage was losing money, and the odds of turning things around didn't seem very bright. But when I laid eyes on Marathon and the Trans-Pecos region, it was love at first sight. I rented a U-Haul as soon as I got home.

If you've never been to the Trans-Pecos, I'm not sure I can really describe it to you. I could say it's empty, desolate, and beautiful. I could say it contains canyons, deserts, ghost towns, the Guadalupe Mountains, Big Bend National Park, and very few inhabitants. But none of that really gets to the heart of the place.

Put it this way: When you cross the Pecos River, you enter a time warp, a place where the traditions of the Old West are still alive. Sure, they've got telephones and gas stations and fast-food joints like the rest of America, but in the Trans-Pecos it's not unusual to see somebody on horseback talking on a cell phone, a pickup pulling a chuck wagon at the gas pump, or a dust-covered cowboy with his spurs on, in line at the Dairy Queen.

The Gage Hotel is smack in the middle of it all. A cattleman named Alfred Gage built the place in the late 1800s. It's a big, red brick building that stands out like a sore thumb in the middle of little Marathon's main street. The old hotel lobby and the restaurant were popular gathering places for all the locals. The whole hotel is decorated with old saddles, branding irons, and other cowboy memorabilia, but for a kid like me, fresh in from the city, the most amazing artifacts were the cowboys who came by for breakfast every morning.

In Houston, I hung around with a lot of kids who called themselves cowboys. They wore fancy snakeskin cowboy boots, big Stetsons with feathers in the hatbands, starched white shirts, and neatly pressed jeans. The cowboys in Marathon wore cowboy boots and hats too, only they had spurs on their boots, and their hats were covered with mud and blood. When they talked to me about roping, I thought they meant the rodeo event. I had done my share of cutting calves in the Fort Worth stockyards, but I had always worked in a hydraulic chute, where you trapped your calf with the push of a button. These guys were actually out riding around on horseback all day, roping and wrassling calves. Hanging around with them was like being an extra in a Western.

I loved being out in the Trans-Pecos and the job was fine, except for the fact that the cook hated me. I was trying to get him to clean the kitchen up and move a little faster during busy periods, but I guess he wasn't interested in taking orders from a smart-ass city kid. In the middle of dinner on my third Saturday night, with fifty people seated in the dining room and another hundred waiting in the lobby for tables, the cook walked out on me.

So I went into the kitchen and starting slinging the hash. That was my introduction to cooking. Actually, the food was so simple that it wasn't really much of a problem. Grilling steaks and hamburgers isn't exactly brain surgery, and there was a pot of

stew and some vegetables already made. I cooked dinner and everybody was happy. Of course, the real problem was that I couldn't find another cook to hire. The only accomplished cooks in the area were making top dollar working at the big ranches.

I was stuck. Either I put on the apron and took over the kitchen at the Gage, or I moved back to Houston. I was too much in love with the Trans-Pecos to give up after only three weeks, so I decided to take up cooking. It wasn't much fun at first. The menu

was pretty boring, and the fact that Marathon is located in the middle of nowhere made it hard to get any interesting ingredients. The locals didn't much mind; they were used to it. But the Gage Hotel attracted a lot of sophisticated people from Houston, Dallas, Fort Worth, Austin, and San Antonio. They stayed at the historic hotel while they visited Big Bend National Park, and they weren't very impressed with my menu. I had lots of ideas from my days working at big city restaurants, but most of them were impossible to carry out. Fresh fish? Baby lettuces? Choice beef? Forget it.

There are no supermarkets in Marathon, and there aren't any butchers, bakeries, farm stands, or dairies either. The only supplies I could get came from a restaurant purveyor's truck that stopped by twice a week. It didn't have many of the things I wanted. Other stuff, like fresh produce, just didn't survive the long trip to Marathon in the heat of West Texas summers. Meanwhile, I had customers like Dan Rather eating hamburgers in my dining room.

So I started looking around. I asked a guy whose garden I admired if he would sell me some tomatoes. And I talked him into planting some other vegetables too. Pretty soon lots of local gardeners were selling me their extra vegetables, and I was happy to buy them. Then I bought a couple of young goats from a local ranch and slaughtered them myself in the backyard. I could have gotten in a lot of trouble for that, but at the time I had no idea about USDA regulations. Everybody loved my *cabrito* stews and *cabrito* enchiladas (*cabrito* is Spanish for kid goat)—soon I became the biggest buyer of goats in the area.

The Gage Hotel catered a lot of outdoor parties at an old watering hole close to Marathon called the Post. Cooking outdoors on a large scale wasn't something I knew much about, so I hired some of the famous cowboy cooks to help me out. They taught me about Dutch oven cooking and baking and shared their recipes for a lot of cowboy camp dishes.

I hired some of the famous local cowboy cooks to help me out. They taught me about Dutch oven cooking and baking and shared their recipes for a lot of cowboy camp dishes.

With the help of the local gardeners, ranchers, and cowboys cooks, the food at the Gage started to improve and, within a few years, it came to be pretty highly regarded. During that time, I went to Santa Fe to visit some of the famous restaurants there. When the chefs and restaurant folks I met there started talking about seeking out fresh local ingredients instead of buying the stuff that came on the purveyor's truck, I had to laugh. I had stumbled into a major trend in Southwestern cooking mainly because, in Marathon, I didn't have a choice.

In 1994, I quit my job at the Gage. I was ready for a change. Al Micallef, a rancher from over near Alpine, was known around the area as a very successful businessman, so one day I asked him for his advice. I told him I wanted to have my own restaurant, and I asked how I should go about it. Within a few weeks Al, his associate Mike Evans, and I were drawing up plans for a new restaurant. We found a property we liked in downtown Alpine. It was an old house, built in the 1880s, with a big patio out back. Designing a kitchen from scratch and having a menu that allowed me to try out some new ideas was a lot of fun. We called the new restaurant Reata, after the ranch in

Giant, and we opened for business on March 5, 1995.

If you've ever read *Giant*, you know the feeling we were trying to capture. We wanted the restaurant to feel like the old ranch house in the book, the kind of place where our regular customers would feel at home with their spurs on. I guess the concept worked pretty well, because the place was packed right from the start.

Through Al and the restaurant, I got to know a lot of the local ranching families around Alpine, and I learned a lot about cooking from visiting their ranches. During roundup, a ranch has to feed a slew of cowboys; during deer season, they have to feed all the hunters; and, of course, there are parties, weddings, and barbecues all the time. Most ranches have huge kitchens in the main house, plus elaborate outdoor kitchens with barbecue smokers, picnic tables, and everything you need to feed a hundred people.

These ain't little family farms. We're talking about ranches of 100,000, 200,000, 300,000 acres. The headquarters at Al's CF Ranch is like a small town. Besides the residences, there's an administration building, a blacksmith shop, garages, helicopter pads, and movie sets—they film a lot of Westerns there. Part of the reason that the restaurant business never got going in the Trans-Pecos is that life always used to revolve around the big ranches, and that's where most of the best cooks worked.

Some ranchers, like Cliff Teinert at the Long X, are very good cooks themselves. Cliff is something of a historical expert on cowboy cooking. He still cooks sometimes at fund-raising dinners for the Ranching Heritage Center in Lubbock. He has a restored chuck wagon from the old XIT Ranch that he was still using until a few years ago, but it was so valuable that somebody convinced him to put it away and save it for a museum. So he built himself a brand new chuck wagon from the wheels up. Cliff used to cater events all over Texas. Cliff taught me all the fine points of cowboy cooking, like how to smoke *cabrito*, how to roast prime rib, and how to make sourdough biscuits.

I always thought of biscuits as something you get with fried chicken at a fast-food drive-through place, but Cliff educated me. He told me that if you can make good biscuits in the Trans-Pecos, you're halfway home. Then all you need is meat. Nobody's very picky about vegetables out here; they'll eat anything you set beside a juicy steak and a tender biscuit. I had never made biscuits before, but, needless to say, learning how to make good biscuits and sourdough rolls quickly became a top priority at the Reata.

Besides the biscuits, the other reason the Reata Restaurant caught on is that, over the last few years, the Trans-Pecos has changed. There are more visitors now than ever before. Lots of people have always visited Big Bend National Park, sixty miles to the

south, but they used to camp in the park. Now they are touring the whole area, staying in hotels, and eating in restaurants.

Some of the old-timers don't like having all these tourists around. To them, two cars on the same road is a traffic jam. But most of the local folks we see at the Reata are pretty happy about the influx of tourists and about having lively restaurants and bars to hang out in. Checking out the tourists gives the locals a reason to come into town. The local characters in their dirty cowboy hats, with their spurs jangling come in to gawk at the out-of-towners, and the out-of-towners come in to gawk at all the colorful Western characters. It's pretty amusing for everybody.

In the summer of 1995, *The Streets of Laredo* and a couple of other movies were filmed around Alpine. During the shoots, a lot of movie stars and Hollywood types came into the Reata all the time. Maybe they hung out here because of the movie theme, maybe it was because they were shooting Westerns, or maybe it was because there aren't too many other places to eat around here.

Whatever brought them in, we never made a big deal about it. We don't put celebrities' pictures on the walls, and the locals, being mostly West Texas cowboys, don't go in much for autographs or oohing and aahing. (To tell you the truth, I think the real cowboys expected the movie star cowboys to come over and ask for their autographs.) I guess the low-key atmosphere made the movie folk comfortable. But the all-star clientele did get the attention of the press. Reporters who came to write about the movies visited the restaurant, and pretty soon magazines like *Martha Stewart Living*, *Travel and Leisure*, and *Texas Monthly* were doing flattering stories about our food. Before long the Reata became pretty famous, for a little restaurant in the middle of nowhere.

By the time stories about Reata started turning up in food magazines, I realized that the name we had come up with for our cooking style, West Texas cowboy cuisine, wasn't as original as we thought it was. According to an article I read, Robert Del Grande in Houston invented the name "cowboy cuisine" for his own cooking style. I've eaten in Robert's famous restaurant, Cafe Annie, and I hope to eat there again sometime soon: It's one of the best restaurants in Texas.

Of course, there's a difference between what Robert Del Grande calls cowboy cuisine and what I call cowboy cuisine. Robert's food is more elegant and more inventive than what I cook. Robert makes incredible quail roasted in cinnamon; I fry quail in beer batter. Robert roasts a steak in coffee grounds; I put coffee in my redeye gravy. It's kind of like the difference between Houston cowboys and Alpine cowboys. His cowboy cuisine wears a coat and tie with ostrich-skin boots; mine is in dirty jeans and scuffed-up ropers. Anyway, having more than one chef cooking cowboy cuisine is a good thing—before you know it, we'll have a movement on our hands.

> ... having more than one chef cooking cowboy cuisine is a good thing—before you know it, we'll have a movement on our hands.

In fact, I feel like I've got a movement on my hands already. Bob Semple, a banker from Fort Worth, decided to stop by the Reata for a visit in November of 1995. I guess he liked his steak pretty well, because afterwards he asked us if we'd like to build another Reata on top of the Bank One Tower in downtown Fort Worth.

We worked out a deal, took over half of the thirty-fifth floor of the building, and opened for business in the spring of 1996. We also hired some other very talented chefs to man the kitchens at the Reata in Fort Worth. These highly trained culinary pros helped me expand the menu and taught me what a mandolin is (it's a French slicing gizmo). Many of the recipes in this cookbook are a result of those collaborations.

Fort Worth always was a cowboy town. The city fell in love with our meat and biscuits, no-nonsense chuck-wagon cooking, and the whole Trans-Pecos mystique we brought along with us from Alpine. Business was pretty good, so we doubled the size of the restaurant.

Now the Reata, Fort Worth, occupies a whole floor of a skyscraper and has two bars, sixty-five tables, five private dining rooms, and a retail store. It also has floor-to-ceiling glass windows so you can look out over the city.

Sometimes, when things get crazy in the kitchen, I go take a break in the library—a cozy little dining room with windows that face north. I sit in there and stare out over the Fort Worth stockyards in the distance. It helps me keep things in perspective to remember where I came from.

1

Scorching a Steak

A BIG, THICK, CHAR-GRILLED T-BONE, a pile of hot mashed potatoes, and an ice-cold Lone Star beer—that's my idea of West Texas cowboy cuisine. Lots of highly trained chefs wouldn't be caught dead serving this kind of simple, old-fashioned American food in their restaurants, but I get away with it because I'm not really a chef. I'm just a cowboy in the kitchen.

One of the editors of Martha Stewart's magazine came out to visit us one time. She was shocked by all the red meat, butter, and cream in my recipes and by the way we heap things on a plate. I guess it's been quite a while since anybody ate that way in New York. "Your menu is such a throw back it seems new," she told me.

She was right; my cooking really is a throwback. Steak and potatoes, buttermilk biscuits, bacon-wrapped shrimp—these were all standards on Texas tables in the 1950s. I wasn't trying to make a statement or start a back-to-the-past movement in cooking when I started serving this stuff. I like this food and frankly, at the time, I didn't know how to cook anything else. The miracle is that everybody else seems to love these foods too—even the Martha Stewart editor cleaned her plate. Maybe it's nostalgia that makes this food taste so good. Or maybe we've just been trying too hard for the last fifty years.

That I never really set out to be a chef has turned out to be an advantage in some ways. It's given me the freedom to keep things simple. I learned what I know about food hanging around campfires with cowboy cooks. Scorching a steak over hot coals was their idea of gourmet cooking.

The old doughpunchers have a different way of thinking about cooking. One cook told me that the reason they called black southern cooking "soul food" was because they never had all the ingredients they needed, so they always had to add a little bit of their soul to make up for what was missing. That's the way I like to think about cowboy cooking. It's kind of like western soul food. It was shaped by what they had to cook with, but also by what was missing.

What they had was a lot of beef and simple staples like flour, potatoes, beans, and cornmeal, plus whatever they could find along the trail. What they didn't have was just about everything else. Western cooking evolved from this short list of ingredients, and, for better or worse, this cuisine of scarcity has shaped West Texas tastes. If you grew up in France, maybe you dream about snails in garlic butter when you lie in bed at night. If you grew up in West Texas, you would have the same dreams about steak and mashed potatoes.

I think the other reason my outdated food seems so new is because I don't make much of an effort to serve low-fat stuff. Granted, steak and potatoes is not on anybody's health-food hit parade, but that's another part of the tradition. Cowboys lived on beans and biscuits and other such health foods most of the week. When a cowboy went into town for dinner on Friday night, he was looking for a big thick steak. If you eat a low-fat, high-fiber diet yourself most of the time, I'm sure you know the feeling.

Steak isn't for every meal. It's a special event, a big treat. So while you're eating one of these steaks or chops, think of it as your reward for eating beans and biscuits all week.

Grilled Strip Steak with Cilantro Butter

YIELD: 4 SERVINGS

They call this a New York strip in Kansas City and a Kansas City strip in New York. The strip steak, or top loin, is the cut that forms the bigger side of a porterhouse or T-bone. Since you've got to fire up the grill anyway, you might as well serve this steak with Char-Grilled Squash (page 115).

$^1/_4$ cup Worcestershire sauce
$^1/_4$ cup olive oil
4 strip steaks (about 14 ounces each)
4 teaspoons Reata Grill Blend (page 200)
4 slices Cilantro Butter (page 202)

✪ Prepare and heat a grill. ✪ Mix the Worcestershire sauce and olive oil in a shallow pan. ✪ Soak the steaks in this mixture while the grill is heating. ✪ Remove from marinade and season with Reata Grill Blend. When the grill feels hot to a hand held 5 inches over the fire, it is ready to use. ✪ Place the steaks on the grill and cook them for 5 minutes on each side for medium. ✪ Top each steak with a cold slice of Cilantro Butter. ✪ Serve immediately.

Char-Grilled Texas T-Bone with Caciotta Cheese Enchiladas

YIELD: 4 SERVINGS

I once cooked meals on a luxury train trip that went from Fort Worth to Chihuahua City, Mexico. After the train trip, I'd stop into a little coffee shop down there that had a T-bone steak on the menu. The steak wasn't bad, but it was grilled without any seasonings so I'd order their cheese enchiladas on the side. I liked the combination so much I started serving this dish at the Reata.

8 Caciotta Cheese Enchiladas (page 42)
4 T-bone steaks (about 16 ounces each)
2 tablespoons olive oil
2 tablespoons Reata Grill Blend (page 200)
Kosher salt to taste
Freshly ground pepper to taste

✪ Prepare the enchiladas and heat the grill. ✪ Rub the steaks with the oil and seasonings and set aside at room temperature while grill heats. When the grill feels medium-hot when you hold your hand 5 inches over the fire, it is ready to use. ✪ Place the steaks on the grill and cook them for 5 minutes on each side for medium. ✪ At serving time, place the steaks on 4 plates and top each steak with 2 hot Caciotta Cheese Enchiladas. ✪ Serve immediately.

Char-Grilled
Texas T-Bone

Char-Grilled Texas T-bone with Caciotta Cheese Enchiladas

Pepper-Crusted Tenderloin with Port

YIELD: 4 SERVINGS

Steaks cut from the tenderloin are also called filet mignon, Chateaubriand, and lots of other French names. Whatever you call them, tenderloin steaks should be at least two inches thick. I like mine about the size of a base-ball. If you don't want to make the Roasted Shallots before you cook this dish, just throw a whole minced shallot in with the steaks. Sop up the wine sauce with Blue Cheese Mashed Potatoes (page 109).

$^1/_3$ cup Cracked Peppercorns (page 199)

Kosher salt to taste

4 beef tenderloin steaks (10 to 12 ounces each)

3 tablespoons vegetable oil

2 cups port

2 tablespoons Roasted Shallots (page 198)
   or 1 large shallot, minced

3 tablespoons honey

3 tablespoons butter

✪ Preheat the oven to 500°. ✪ Press the salt and pepper evenly into the surfaces of the steaks. ✪ Heat the oil in a large, heavy sauté pan over high heat. ✪ Place the steaks in the pan without crowding (this may have to be done in batches), and cook them, uncovered, for 3 minutes on each side. ✪ Remove the steaks to a sheet pan and place them in the oven to finish cooking, about 8 minutes for medium rare. ✪ While the steaks are in the oven, pour the port into the pan the steaks were cooked in and reduce by half. ✪ Add the shallots and honey and stir until they are well blended. ✪ Remove the steaks from the oven and allow them to rest for 5 minutes. ✪ Whisk the butter into the port mixture and add salt to taste. ✪ Place each steak on a plate, pour the port sauce evenly over the steaks, and serve.

Chipotle Meatloaf

YIELD: 8 SERVINGS

A chipotle is a smoked jalapeño. The fleshy jalapeño is hard to air dry, so ancient Mexicans figured out a way to preserve the peppers with wood smoke. The smoke-flavored pepper gives a new dimension to meatloaf. Look for canned chipotles in adobo sauce at Hispanic grocery stores. Serve the meatloaf with Corn Pudding Pie (page 121).

2 pounds ground chuck
1 cup diced red bell pepper
1 cup finely chopped onion
2 scallions, thinly sliced
2 tablespoons Roasted Garlic (page 198)
    or 5 cloves garlic, minced
1 chipotle pepper
1 tablespoon adobo sauce reserved from
    the chipotle can
1 tablespoon Worcestershire sauce
3 eggs
$^1/_2$ cup bread crumbs
1 teaspoon Reata Grill Blend (page 200)
Kosher salt to taste
Freshly ground pepper to taste

✪ Preheat the oven to 350°. ✪ Mix all of the ingredients in a large bowl. ✪ Shape the mixture and put it in a loaf pan (approximately $8^1/_2$ by $4^1/_2$ by $2^1/_2$ inches). ✪ Cover the loaf with foil and bake for 1 to $1^1/_4$ hours. ✪ Remove the foil toward the end of the baking time if you want the top of the loaf to brown. ✪ When the meatloaf is finished baking, remove it from the oven and let it stand for 15 minutes before serving. ✪ Unmold the loaf and slice it into serving pieces. ✪ Serve warm.

Variation
Chipotle Chorizo Meatloaf: For an even spicier meatloaf, use $1^1/_2$ pounds of ground chuck and $^1/_2$ pound of Chihuahuan Chorizo (page 48).

A Cattleman's Guide to Beef Buying

★ ★ ★ ★ ★ ★ ★ ★ ★ ★ ★ ★ ★ ★ ★ ★ ★ ★ ★ ★

Branded beef is available at most good supermarkets, and it's your best bet for getting a good steak at home. Certified Hereford, Certified Angus, Coleman, and Sterling Silver are some of the brand names you might see at your store's meat counter. Brand-name meat may sound like a strange idea, but to understand the reasoning behind it, you have to take a look at what's happened to the USDA grading system.

A decade ago, the low-fat food trend started seriously hurting beef sales. So the cattle industry called for a change in the way that beef was being graded. Responding to the public's demand for leaner beef, in 1987 USDA Good, the third class of beef under Prime and Choice, was renamed USDA Select. Things haven't been the same since.

"Over the last twenty years, the beef industry has started feeding cattle differently in order to produce leaner beef," says Molly Patterson of the National Cattleman's Beef Association. "American beef is 27 percent leaner today than it was twenty years ago. As a result, the production of USDA Prime is down. The highest level of USDA Prime isn't even produced anymore."

Now that the average American consumer has become so paranoid about fat, we are paying a premium for poorer quality beef. Cattlemen, in turn, are being pushed to produce more of it, and the result is a drastic decline in the quality of all grades of beef.

Marbling is what makes the difference in the flavor of beef. Prime is roughly 15 percent more marbled than Choice, and Choice is about 15 percent more marbled than Select. If you're on a diet you eat Select, and if you want a really good steak you buy Choice, since Prime has all but disappeared. Sounds easy enough. But it's not.

USDA Choice is a very, very broad category. There are actually three different levels of quality within the Choice grade, usually called "small marbling, modest marbling, and moderate marbling." Moderately marbled USDA Choice is the top of the heap, just one step short of Prime. Unfortunately, the USDA doesn't label moderately marbled Choice any differently than the small marbled variety. So how do you know you've got your hands on some moderately marbled Choice?

That's where the branded beef programs come in. "The branded beef programs go beyond government grading," says Molly Patterson. After the USDA issues a grade, the brand-name graders come through and stamp the meat that fits their program. What they are really doing, by and large, is cherry-picking the top third of the USDA Choice category.

By removing the Prime, Choice, and Select labels from the product, the branded beef programs are making it easier to buy good beef. By selecting the most marbled beef that's available, they are also clearing up all the confusion of the USDA grading system.

Grilled Venison Backstrap with Apricot Glaze

YIELD: 4 TO 6 SERVINGS

The backstrap is the venison tenderloin. It deserves to be grilled rare like any good cut of meat. Serve it with baked sweet potatoes cut into rounds, topped with Cook's Butter (page 202).

1 whole venison backstrap

3 tablespoons Reata Grill Blend (page 200)

$^1/_4$ cup white wine

2 cups apricot preserves

2 tablespoons olive oil

✪ Prepare the grill. ✪ Remove any silverskin (the white membrane) from the backstrap. ✪ Cut the backstrap across the grain into thick serving pieces (about 2 inches thick each). ✪ Sprinkle the Reata Grill Blend on the meat. ✪ In a saucepan heat the white wine to boiling and cook until reduced by one half. ✪ Blend in the preserves and cook over medium heat until liquefied. Set aside.

✪ Brush a little olive oil on each piece of meat and place the pieces on the grill. ✪ Cook the meat for about 4 minutes. ✪ Turn it and cook for another 3 minutes. ✪ Brush each piece of meat with the apricot glaze. ✪ When the meat is done to your liking, turn it one more time and brush the other side with the glaze. ✪ Cook until the glaze just begins to bubble (the glaze has to be added at the last minute or it will burn). ✪ Serve immediately.

Lamb Chops with Jalapeño Jelly

YIELD: 4 SERVINGS

Ask your butcher for thick lamb chops if you like them rare. For a great meal, serve these chops on a bed of Creamed Spinach with Texas Tarragon (page 114) and a side of Bacon Cheese Grits (page 122).

2 tablespoons olive oil

Leaves from 3 sprigs of rosemary

2 teaspoons lime juice

4 tablespoons Jalapeño Jelly (page 170)

8 lamb chops, T-bone or loin

Kosher salt to taste

1 tablespoon Cracked Pepper (page 199)

✪ To make the marinade, combine the olive oil, rosemary, lime juice, and Jalapeño Jelly in a bowl and whisk them together. ✪ Place the lamb chops and marinade in a plastic bag. ✪ Remove the air from the bag, seal, and refrigerate for at least 2 hours, or overnight.

✪ Prepare a grill. ✪ Remove the chops from the marinade and season them with salt and pepper. ✪ Place the chops 2 to 3 inches above white coals and cook the meat on both sides (3 to 4 minutes for medium rare) turning frequently so the marinade doesn't burn. ✪ Place 2 chops on each plate and serve warm.

Lamb Chops

Oven-Roasted Tenderloin of Pork with Apple-Poblano Chutney

Oven-Roasted Tenderloin of Pork
with Apple-Poblano Chutney

YIELD: 4 SERVINGS

Reggie Ferguson and Clay Wilson invented this dish at the Reata in Alpine. Pork tenderloins cook fast, so keep an eye on them. Serve with Coyote Chayote (page 128) and Corn-Bread Dressing (page 100).

2 pork tenderloins (about 1 pound each)

3 tablespoons olive oil

Kosher salt to taste

Freshly ground pepper to taste

1 tablespoon unsalted butter

2 sprigs fresh sage leaves, coarsely chopped

2 cups Apple-Poblano Chutney (page 167)

✪ Preheat the oven to 350°. ✪ Prepare the tenderloins by rubbing them with 1 tablespoon of olive oil each. ✪ Season them generously with salt and pepper. ✪ Heat the remaining 1 tablespoon oil and the butter in an ovenproof sauté pan. ✪ Place the tenderloins in the pan and sear them on all sides to a golden brown. ✪ Remove the pan from the heat, sprinkle sage over the meat, and set the pan in the oven. ✪ Roast the tenderloins, turning them once, for about 10 minutes. ✪ Check for doneness. The meat should be just slightly pink but cooked through. ✪ When the tenderloins are finished cooking, remove them from the oven, cover them with foil, and let them rest for 5 minutes before cutting.

✪ At serving time slice the pork tenderloin into thick slices, on the diagonal. ✪ Serve the slices on a big platter with $^1/_2$ cup of chutney on the side.

Refrigerator-Smoked Ribeye with Horseradish Sour Cream

YIELD: 4 SERVINGS

The ribeye is the most marbled of all steaks. Don't be afraid of the big circle of fat in the middle—that's what makes a ribeye tender. Smoking a ribeye and then finishing it in the oven gives it a big flavor.

4 ribeye steaks (about 14 ounces each)
2 tablespoons olive oil
8 teaspoons Reata Grill Blend (page 200)
$1^1/_3$ cups Horseradish Sour Cream (recipe follows)

✪ Prepare an outdoor smoker (see page 31) or follow the directions for indoor smoking, on page 127. ✪ If using a stove-top smoker, place 2 tablespoons of smoking chips in the bottom. ✪ Preheat a broiler and adjust the rack about 8 inches from the heat source. ✪ Rub the steaks with olive oil and sprinkle them generously with Reata Grill Blend. ✪ Place the steaks on the rack in the smoker and set the smoker over high heat. ✪ When smoke begins to appear, seal the smoker, start timing, and reduce the heat to medium. ✪ With steaks that are $1^1/_2$ inches thick, smoke for 7 minutes on a stove-top setup, or 15 to 30 minutes in an outdoor smoker. ✪ Remove the steaks and set them on a sheet pan. ✪ Place the steaks under the broiler for 4 minutes per side for medium rare. ✪ Adjust the time to cook the steaks to your taste. ✪ Remove the steaks from the oven and serve them hot, topped with Horseradish Sour Cream.

HORSERADISH SOUR CREAM

YIELD: $1^3/_4$ CUPS

For a spicier dip, add as much horseradish as you can stand.

$1^1/_2$ cups sour cream
$^1/_4$ cup prepared horseradish
Pinch of paprika
Kosher salt to taste

✪ Combine all of the ingredients in mixing bowl and stir well. ✪ Serve at once or store in a container in the refrigerator for future use.

Refrigerator Smoking and Stove-Top Smokers

★ ★ ★ ★ ★ ★ ★ ★ ★ ★ ★ ★ ★ ★ ★ ★ ★ ★ ★ ★

In the back of the Reata in Alpine, we have an old refrigerator we use for smoking. Using a refrigerator to smoke meat sounds crazy, but we didn't think it up all by ourselves. It's actually an old Texas tradition.

To make a refrigerator smoker, you tear out all the plastic from an old refrigerator, then you drill a slot in the bottom and stick one of those electric charcoal lighters through the hole. You put your meat, fish, or whatever you want to smoke on the refrigerator racks. Then you pile a little bit of hardwood chips on top of the charcoal lighter, plug it in, and shut the door. The door seal keeps the smoke inside, and your food gets a good, strong smoky flavor pretty quickly.

One time, we had a guy working in the kitchen who wasn't too familiar with the process. We sent him out to smoke a prime rib. He filled the refrigerator halfway up with several armloads of hardwood and plugged in the lighter. Flames were shooting six feet above the refrigerator when we went to check on the meat. We had to call the fire department to put out our refrigerator.

Several of the recipes in this cookbook call for refrigerator-smoked ingredients. We don't really expect you to gut an old refrigerator to follow these recipes. Nowadays, there's a much easier and safer alternative to the old refrigerator smoker. It's called a stove-top smoker.

Stove-top smokers were designed in Scandinavia, but some companies in the United States sell them now too. They are sealed stainless-steel containers that you can use on your home stove-top. You sprinkle some of the hardwood sawdust that comes with the cooker on the bottom, place the food on a rack, seal the container, and put it on a burner. In the tightly sealed container, the sawdust smolders without stinking up the house, and your food is smoked in minutes.

The Cameron Smoker Cooker, which comes from an outfit in Colorado, is one we've tried that works great. It comes with apple, alder, cherry, hickory, maple, mesquite, oak, and pecan "smoke dust." To order one or get more information, call them toll free at 888-563-0227, or visit their website at www.cameronsmoker.com

Chicken-Fried Steak with Cracked-Pepper Gravy

YIELD: 4 SERVINGS

Pour the Cracked Pepper Gravy over the steaks and some Garlic Mashed Potatoes (page 108). For a real Texas truck-stop touch, serve Iceberg Quarters with Buttermilk Dressing (page 134) on the side.

FLOUR SPICE

$1^1/_2$ cups flour

2 teaspoons kosher salt

2 teaspoons freshly ground pepper

4 tablespoons paprika

BATTER

2 eggs

$^1/_2$ cup buttermilk, or $^1/_4$ cup of milk mixed with $^1/_4$ cup Sourdough Starter (page 89)

$^1/_2$ cup Shiner Bock or any good bock beer

2 cups peanut oil

4 tenderized round steaks (about $^1/_2$ pound each)

2 cups Cracked Pepper Gravy (page 35)

✪ Prepare the flour spice by blending the flour, salt, pepper, and paprika. ✪ Set aside on a plate or wax paper. ✪ Prepare the batter by mixing the eggs with a whisk, in a large bowl. ✪ Add the buttermilk, or milk and sourdough starter, and beer. ✪ Whisk to blend. Set aside.

✪ In a deep, heavy skillet, heat the oil to 350°. ✪ While the oil is heating, prepare the round steaks by dredging them in the flour spice, taking care to evenly coat the meat. ✪ Shake off any excess. ✪ Dip the meat into the batter, and then again in the flour spice, evenly coating the batter so it is dry on the outside. ✪ When the oil temperature reaches 350° (when a drop of batter sizzles when dropped in it), gently slide one steak into the hot oil. ✪ Cook the steak about 5 minutes. ✪ Turn it, taking care not to break the coating, and cook the meat 5 more minutes, or until the batter is nicely browned. ✪ Drain the cooked steak on paper towels. ✪ Repeat with the other steaks. ✪ Hold the cooked steaks in a 225° oven until all four are done. ✪ Pour Cracked-Pepper Gravy over the steaks and serve.

Chicken-Fried Steak with Cracked-Pepper Gravy

Calf Fries with Cracked-Pepper Gravy

YIELD: 4 SERVINGS

During spring roundup, while castrating calves, the cowboys like to roast the calf testicles over hot coals. The testicles burst open while cooking, and you eat them like oysters, which is why these "calf fries" are also known as "mountain oysters." The old vaqueros said they'd make you strong as a bull.

BATTER

2 eggs

1/2 cup buttermilk

1/2 cup Shiner Bock beer or any
   good bock beer

2 cups peanut oil

36 calf fries, cleaned of
   membranes
   (How? Ask your butcher.)

Flour Spice (page 32)

2 cups Cracked-Pepper Gravy
   (page 35)

✪ Prepare the batter by mixing eggs with a whisk in a large bowl. ✪ Add the buttermilk and beer. ✪ Whisk to blend. ✪ Set aside.

✪ In a deep, heavy skillet, heat the oil to 350°. ✪ While the oil is heating, prepare the calf fries by dredging them in the flour spice, taking care to evenly coat. ✪ Shake off any excess flour. ✪ Dip the calf fries into the batter, and then again in the flour spice, evenly coating the batter so it is dry on the outside. ✪ When the oil temperature reaches 350° (when a drop of batter sizzles when dropped in it), gently slide 12 calf fries into the hot oil. ✪ Cook about 3 minutes. ✪ Turn them, taking care not to break the coating, and cook them 3 more minutes or until the batter is nicely browned. ✪ Drain the cooked calf fries on paper towels. ✪ Repeat for the other two batches. ✪ Hold the cooked calf fries in a 225° oven until all 3 batches are done. ✪ Serve with Cracked-Pepper Gravy (page 35).

Cracked-Pepper Gravy

YIELD: ABOUT 3 CUPS

This is Reata's jazzed-up version of old-fashioned cream gravy.

$1/_4$ cup unsalted butter

5 tablespoons flour

$2^1/_2$ cups milk

$1^1/_2$ teaspoons kosher salt

4 teaspoons Cracked Pepper
  (see page 199)

✪ Melt the butter in a heavy saucepan. When the foam goes down, whisk in the flour. ✪ Continually whisk until the flour cooks, becoming a fragrant light brown. ✪ Slowly add the milk, continuing to whisk to keep lumps from forming. ✪ Season with salt and pepper. ✪ Simmer gravy for 10 minutes to cook and reduce. ✪ Serve hot.

2

Chili con Carne and
the Old Cocineros

THE MEXICANS TAUGHT US TEXANS EVERYTHING we know about being cow-boys and most of what we know about cooking. In the old days, folks rode back and forth between northern Mexico and South Texas all the time without any fuss about international borders. In the Trans-Pecos, we still do.

Boquillas, Mexico, is in the state of Chihuahua, across the Rio Grande from Big Bend National Park. I go over there all the time to visit my buddy Jose Falcon's little restaurant. I remember one time some folks came in from Los Angeles, and I thought it would be fun to take them over to Jose's.

To get to Boquillas, you go down to the riverbank and whistle for an hombre on the other side to come over in a rowboat and get you. The river isn't more than a hundred yards across there, so it's no big boat trip. Then on the other side, you rent a burro or a horse for a couple of bucks and ride the mile or so into town—no customs, no border guard, no nothing. Main street in Boquillas is a rutted dirt road with one tequila bar and Jose's little restaurant, which is actually just the front porch of his house set up with ten tables. You should have seen those cool Hollywood types, with their three-hundred-dollar sunglasses and their sweaters tied around their waists, riding those dusty burros into town. I wish I'd had a camera.

The food at Jose's place is mostly tacos and *chalupas,* refried beans—the usual stuff. The Californians asked me if this kind of food was just for the tourists. I guess they were expecting some elaborate dishes like you'd get in Mexico City or something. But Chihuahua is as different from Mexico City as the Trans-Pecos is from Los Angeles. And the Mexican food on that side of the river tastes pretty much like the Mexican food on this side of the river.

I've read some Mexican cookbooks that make a big deal about how bad Tex-Mex food is. They make it sound like chili con carne is some kind of evil plot. The Mexican *cocineros* who invented chili con carne in the cattle camps were just throwing tough cuts of beef and chiles together in the same pot because that's what they had on hand. I don't think the concept of authentic Mexican cuisine was really on their minds all that much.

In the beginning of the cowboy era, the cooks were mostly from south of the border, and the food was pretty much the same stuff they cooked over in Chihuahua. That changed when the cattle business started making money and lots of Anglo ranchers moved in. White flour, lard, bacon, and other gringo staples started turning up in cowboy cooking. But most of the basics, like frijoles, chile peppers, and Mexican seasonings, remained the same. A lot of the best dishes in cowboy cooking are crossbreeds, combinations of Mexican and American ingredients. The old *cocineros* would laugh themselves to tears if they could hear people today debating about whether or not chili con carne is really Mexican food.

At the Reata restaurants, we jumble up our own Mexican combo plates with the same disregard for authenticity. We serve steaks with enchiladas, savory bread pudding with chorizo, and apple crisp with Mexican *cajeta* caramel sauce. This food has nothing in common with the stuff they eat in Mexico City. And, as long as it tastes good, who cares?

Red Chile Sauce

YIELD: ABOUT 3 CUPS

This is a classic red sauce that can be used for any kind of enchiladas.

2 cups Red Chile Paste (see page 197)
1 cup diced tomato
1 teaspoon ground cumin
1 tablespoon honey
Kosher salt to taste
2 tablespoons oil

✪ Place the chile paste, tomato, cumin, and honey in a blender and purée until smooth. ✪ Adjust seasonings with salt. ✪ Heat the oil in a skillet over medium-high heat. ✪ Pour in the purée and cook it for 3 minutes, until the flavors are well combined. ✪ Use the sauce immediately on enchiladas, or store in a glass container in the refrigerator until ready to use. ✪ Keeps for 1 week.

Venison Chili

YIELD: 6 SERVINGS

Chili cook-off winners all have their secret recipes, and many cooks swear that venison makes the best chili. Whether that's true or not, chili is a great way to use tougher game cuts like venison shoulder. Be sure to cut the meat into very small chunks (about the size of the last joint of your little finger). Serve with hot tamales and crackers or Yaller Bread with Pintos (page 98).

$^1/_4$ cup oil

$1^1/_2$ pounds venison chili meat

1 cup Red Chile Paste (see page 197)

1 red onion, chopped

2 tablespoons Roasted Garlic (see page 198)
   or minced garlic

1 tablespoon Pasilla Powder (see page 196)
   or chili powder

2 teaspoons kosher salt

1 tablespoon Tabasco™ Jalapeño Sauce

1 teaspoon Mexican oregano

1 teaspoon ground cumin

3 cups chicken stock

✪ Heat the oil in a stew pot. ✪ Add the chili meat and cook it until it is browned. ✪ Add the chile paste, onion, roasted or minced garlic, pasilla powder, salt, Tabasco™ Jalapeño sauce, oregano, and cumin. ✪ Cook for 5 minutes, or until the onion is wilted. Add the chicken stock and simmer for 45 minutes to 1 hour, or until the venison is tender. ✪ Serve hot.

Venison Chili

Caciotta Cheese Enchiladas

YIELD: 4 SERVINGS

Paula Lambert's Mozzarella Company, in Dallas, makes some of the best handmade cheeses in the country. Her caciotta is a Texas version of Monterey Jack, and it makes a great cheese enchilada. We serve these enchiladas on top of a T-bone at Reata, but they're also good for lunch, with a salad, or for breakfast, with a fried egg on top.

$^1/_3$ cup vegetable oil

8 (8-inch) corn tortillas

2 cups Red Chile Sauce (page 39)

4 $^1/_2$ cups (about $^3/_4$ pound) grated caciotta
    or Monterey Jack cheese

✪ Lightly grease an $11^3/_4$ by 7 $^1/_2$- inch glass baking pan. ✪ Set aside. ✪ Heat the oil in a small skillet over low heat, until it's hot enough to sizzle when a tiny piece of tortilla is dropped in. ✪ Using tongs, dip a tortilla into the hot oil, removing it quickly and letting excess oil drip off. ✪ Dip tortilla into the chile sauce and lay it on a flat surface. ✪ Sprinkle $^1/_2$ cup of the cheese down the center of the tortilla and roll the tortilla from one end to the other. ✪ Lay the enchilada in the prepared pan with the seam down. Repeat the steps with each tortilla, fitting them tightly into the pan. ✪ Pour the remaining chile sauce over the top of the enchiladas and sprinkle them with the remaining cheese. ✪ Prepare these as close to serving time as possible. To finish the enchiladas, preheat the oven to 400° and bake them for 12 minutes. ✪ Serve at once.

The Terlingua Chili Cook-Off is one of the most popular events in the Trans-Pecos. It was started by Dallas food writer Frank X. Tolbert in 1967 to promote his book, *A Bowl of Red*. Some people say that the chili cook-off is what launched the tourist business in the Trans-Pecos. The event also spawned dozens of other chili cook-offs around the country. Nowadays, chili cooks have to win a qualifying event to even participate in the big cook-off in Terlingua. Needless to say, the event has made the Trans-Pecos the world's chili headquarters. The Terlingua chili cook-off is held on the first Saturday in November in the tiny ghost town of Terlingua. If you plan on going, find a place to stay well in advance.

Chicken Burritos with Mushrooms and Sundried Tomato—Goat Cheese Pesto

YIELD: 4 BURRITOS

My wife Sara invented this dish, and it's still one of her favorite dinners. We serve this at Reata with Corn Pudding Pie (page 121).

2 tablespoons olive oil

$^3/_4$ pound boneless and skinless chicken thigh meat, cut into 2-inch dice

$^1/_2$ teaspoon dried ground cumin

Kosher salt to taste

Freshly ground pepper to taste

$^1/_2$ pound sliced fresh mushrooms

$1^1/_2$ cups Sundried Tomato-Goat Cheese Pesto (page 169)

4 (12-inch) flour tortillas

4 heaping tablespoons sour cream

4 heaping tablespoons Pickled Pico de Gallo (page 164)

✪ Heat the oil in a sauté pan and add the chicken. ✪ Add the cumin, salt, and pepper and toss well. ✪ Add the mushrooms. ✪ Sauté over medium heat, stirring often, until the chicken is cooked through (about 6 minutes). ✪ Blend in the pesto and stir until well combined. Remove from heat.

✪ Lay the tortillas out on a flat surface and divide the chicken mixture, allowing one fourth of the filling per tortilla. ✪ Line the chicken filling down the center of each tortilla and fold the top and bottom edges in toward the center. ✪ Roll the two outer edges toward the center, enclosing the mixture. ✪ The finished burrito will be about 9 inches by 3 inches. ✪ Lay each burrito down on a baking pan, seam-side down, and heat in a 225° oven for 5 minutes before serving. ✪ Garnish each burrito with 1 heaping tablespoon sour cream and 1 heaping tablespoon Pico de Gallo. ✪ Serve hot.

Chicken Chile Rellenos

Chicken Chile Rellenos

Chicken
Chile
Rellenos

YIELD: 4 SERVINGS

I was never crazy about Mexican peppers that are stuffed with ground beef and batter-fried. Chicken makes a better pepper stuffing, in my opinion, and stuffed peppers taste better without the batter. At the Reata, we serve these on Cow Camp Creamed Corn (page 113).

CHICKEN STUFFING

1 tablespoon olive oil

1 pound boneless and skinless chicken thigh meat

$1^3/_4$ cups diced tomatoes

$^1/_2$ cup Red Chile Sauce (page 39)

Kosher salt to taste

Freshly ground pepper to taste

4 large poblano peppers, roasted and peeled (see page 195)

2 cups (about 8 ounces) grated Monterey Jack

$^1/_2$ cup (about 2 ounces) goat cheese, crumbled

✪ To prepare the chicken stuffing, heat the oil in a sauté pan and add the chicken. ✪ Sauté the meat over medium heat, turning it several times, until it is cooked through. ✪ Remove the chicken from the heat, and allow it to cool. ✪ Coarsely chop the meat, and put it in a bowl. ✪ Add the tomatoes, chile sauce, salt, and pepper. ✪ Mix gently.

✪ Preheat oven to 350°. ✪ Slit the peppers lengthwise and carefully remove the seeds. Put one quarter of the chicken mixture in each pepper, with the cut side facing up. ✪ Place the peppers on a lightly oiled sheet pan. ✪ Mix together the Monterey Jack and goat cheese and divide it evenly among the peppers, piling cheese on top of the chicken mixture. ✪ Bake the peppers for 20 minutes or until filling is heated through and cheese is melted and bubbling. ✪ Serve at once.

Chorizo con Queso

YIELD: 4 CUPS

This sausage-and-cheese appetizer is usually eaten rolled up in warm flour tortillas, but you can also use it as a tortilla chip dip or as a side dish with scrambled eggs.

1 tablespoon corn oil

$^1/_2$ pound Chihuahuan Chorizo (page 48)

$^1/_2$ cup minced white onion

1 clove garlic, minced

1 cup diced tomato

$^1/_3$ cup Roasted Poblano, diced (see page 195)

$^1/_3$ cup chicken stock

3 cups grated mild Cheddar

✪ Warm the oil in a heavy saucepan over medium heat. ✪ Add the chorizo and cook it for 2 minutes, or until the fat begins to melt. ✪ Add the onion and garlic. ✪ Cook until the chorizo is well browned. ✪ Drain off the grease. ✪ Add the tomato, chile, and chicken stock. ✪ Bring the mixture to a simmer and slowly add cheese, blending it with a spoon. ✪ As each batch of cheese melts, add more, cooking over low heat. ✪ When the cheese has melted and the mixture comes together, it is ready to serve. ✪ Keep warm while serving.

Chorizo con Queso

Chihuahuan Chorizo

YIELD: ABOUT 3 POUNDS

Across the river, in Chihuahua, they love to fry up this spicy Mexican sausage and then mix in some scrambled eggs. Chorizo is also a great flavoring for savory bread puddings (see page 101). You can buy chorizo in a Mexican grocery store, or use this recipe to make your own.

2 ¹/₂ pounds ground pork
1 tablespoon kosher salt
1 teaspoon cracked pepper (page 199)
6 cloves garlic, minced
8 tablespoons Pasilla Powder (page 196)
1 cup chicken stock
1 cup red wine vinegar

✪ Combine all ingredients thoroughly in a large mixing bowl. ✪ Use immediately in a recipe or divide it into several freezer bags and store it in the freezer until needed. ✪ The chorizo must be cooked before serving.

Cabrito Picadillo and Mashed Potato Burritos

YIELD: 4 BURRITOS

In traditional Mexican cooking, cabrito (kid goat) is cooked for a long time over slow heat. But if you mince cabrito meat and sauté it over high heat, it makes an unbeatable picadillo. You can substitute $^3/_4$ pound minced lean pork for the cabrito.

PICADILLO

2 tablespoons oil

$^3/_4$ pound cabrito, minced

2 cloves garlic, minced

$^1/_2$ onion, chopped

1 jalapeño, seeded and chopped

1 tomato, chopped

2 tablespoons Red Chile Paste
  (see page 197)

Juice of $^1/_2$ lime

2 tablespoons chopped fresh
  cilantro leaves

BURRITOS

4 (12-inch) flour tortillas

2 cups Garlic Mashed Potatoes,
  warm (page 108)

4 heaping tablespoons sour cream

4 heaping tablespoons Pickled
  Pico de Gallo (page 164)

✪ To make the picadillo, heat the oil in a skillet over high heat. ✪ Add the cabrito, garlic, onion, and jalapeño. ✪ Cook for 6 minutes, or until the meat is browned. ✪ Add the tomato, chile paste, and lime juice and cook for 4 minutes or until the mixture thickens slightly. ✪ Sprinkle with cilantro.

✪ To make the burritos, lay the tortillas out on a flat surface. ✪ Line $^1/_2$ cup of mashed potatoes down the center of each tortilla and top with $^1/_2$ cup of picadillo. ✪ Fold the top and bottom edges in toward the center. ✪ Roll the two outer edges toward the center enclosing the mixture. The finished burrito will be about 9 inches by 3 inches. ✪ Lay each burrito down on a baking pan, seam-side down, and heat them in a 225° oven for 5 minutes before serving. ✪ Garnish each burrito with 1 heaping tablespoon sour cream and 1 heaping tablespoon Pico de Gallo. ✪ Serve hot.

Crispy Cabrito Ribs

YIELD: SERVES 4 AS AN APPETIZER

Braising the ribs for three hours and then allowing them to cool is the key to getting really crispy cabrito ribs. Crispy cabrito ribs are a delicacy around Junction, Texas, the capital of the Texas goat market.

2 racks of ribs from a cabrito or adult goat
20 peppercorns
2 sprigs thyme
1 stick cinnamon
1 bay leaf
1 cup Jalapeño Jelly (page 170)

✪ Preheat the oven to 300°. Submerge the ribs in water in a roasting pan. ✪ Add the peppercorns, thyme, cinnamon, and bay leaf. ✪ Cover with aluminum foil. ✪ Cook for $2^1/_2$ hours. ✪ Remove from the oven. ✪ Cut away the fat cap from the ribs, if still attached. ✪ Allow the ribs to cool in the refrigerator for at least 30 minutes, or overnight.

✪ When you're ready to serve the ribs, turn the oven to broil, and cut in between the bones to make individual ribs. ✪ Glaze the ribs with Jalapeño Jelly. ✪ Return the ribs to the oven and broil them, turning as needed, for 15 minutes, or until very crispy.

Crispy
Cabrito Ribs

Crispy Cabrito Ribs

Cowboys and Cabrito

★ ★

Spanish shepherds raised sheep for wool, cattle for money, and goats for meat. The Spanish first brought cattle, sheep, and goats to Texas in the 1600s, when the first missions were founded. By 1765, a Spanish census counted tens of thousands of cattle, sheep, and goats roaming the rangelands of southern Texas.

The early *pastores*, or shepherds, stayed with their flocks and kept predators at bay. As the herds and distances increased, they began to do their work on horseback. The mounted shepherds became known as *vaqueros*. (The word was formed from the Spanish roots: *vaca*, "cow," and the suffix *-eros*, meaning "men of," as in rancheros.)

The switch from walking to riding required some changes in shepherd clothing styles. Boots designed for the stirrup, spurs, lariats, large-brimmed hats, and bandanas were all invented by the vaqueros. The vaqueros prided themselves on their ability to live off the land while they herded cattle. They seldom ate beef, but often killed goats when they needed meat.

After the missions were abandoned, the longhorn cattle, sheep, and Spanish goats roamed wild. By the end of the Civil War, there were some three million longhorn cattle in Texas. The Texas cattle business began when "cow hunters" rounded up all the wild cattle they could handle, drove them across the Plains, and sold them at substantial profits in New Mexico and Colorado. The early English-speaking cowboys were known as "buckaroos," which is how they mispronounced the Mexican word *vaqueros*

These early Texan cowboys adopted the clothing, saddlery, and roping techniques of the vaqueros. They also lived off the land and ate the same sort of food. A few cowboys out "cow hunting" couldn't eat a whole longhorn—and besides longhorns were worth a lot of money, but a kid goat (*cabrito* in Spanish) was just the right amount of meat for dinner.

Goat meat has remained a favorite of cowboys to this day, which makes cabrito eating a Texas culinary tradition that's more than three hundred years old.

But Texans and Mexicans aren't the only people who eat cabrito. Moslems, Haitians, Jamaicans, West Africans, and Latin Americans have turned New York City into the nation's largest consumer of goat meat. Nowadays, you can find cabrito in Middle Eastern, Caribbean, and Latino meat markets and grocery stores around the U.S.

Cabrito Picadillo Quesadillas

YIELD: 4 SERVINGS

The combination of spicy goat meat picadillo and creamy goat cheese makes an unbelievable quesadilla. Try these with frozen margaritas or a cold Lone Star beer.

4 (10-inch) flour tortillas
$^3/_4$ cup grated Monterey Jack
$^1/_4$ cup soft goat cheese
Cabrito Picadillo (page 49)
4 teaspoons butter
2 cups Smoked Tomato Guacamole (page 139)

✪ Lay the tortillas out on a flat surface. ✪ Divide $^1/_4$ of the Jack cheese and $^1/_4$ of the goat cheese onto one side of each. ✪ Divide the picadillo evenly over the cheese. ✪ Fold the tortilla over and press lightly until it sticks together. ✪ Melt 1 teaspoon of butter in a skillet and slide in a stuffed tortilla. ✪ Cook for 3 minutes, or until the tortilla is brown and crisp. ✪ Turn and cook 3 minutes on the other side, or until both sides are crisp and the cheese is melted. ✪ Repeat for each quesadilla. ✪ Cut each folded tortilla into 3 wedges and serve with Smoked Tomato Guacamole on the side.

3

Chuck-Wagon Game Birds and Seafood

ROBB AND I STOPPED BY THE LONG X RANCH one day and found Cliff Teinert out by the chuck wagon. He had twenty deer hunters staying at the ranch, and they ate all of their meals there.

"What'd ya'll have for breakfast?" I asked out of idle curiosity.

"Skip made fried quail with biscuits and gravy," he replied matter-of-factly. Skip Rhodes is the chuck-wagon cook at the Long X, and just the thought of his fried quail with biscuits and gravy made my mouth water.

Some people seem surprised at the idea of cowboys eating quail, trout, and other such fancy-sounding foods, but hunting and fishing have always been part of cowboy culture. It's a tradition handed down from the vaqueros, who never killed a livestock animal if they could find wild game to eat instead. Game birds and fresh fish were kind of a bonus meal, a special treat that cowboys got to eat when they got lucky. Fish and game birds were especially popular with bacon, biscuits, and coffee in the morning, since breakfast was usually the most boring meal of the day.

Seafood, like redfish, oysters, and shrimp, was never common in the Trans-Pecos. But in some outfits, like the King Ranch, located in the coastal plains between Corpus Christi and Brownsville, seafood is an everyday ingredient of meals.

Some people seem surprised at the idea of cowboys eating quail and trout and other such fancy-sounding foods, but hunting and fishing have always been part of cowboy culture.

Batter-fried quail is one of our most popular items at the Reata restaurants, but we're not open for breakfast, so we serve quail as an appetizer. After I visited Cliff that morning, I thought about fried quail with biscuits and gravy for the rest of the day. I must have dreamed about them too. The next morning, I got up and went straight down to the restaurant. I fried up a huge batch of quail for Robb, myself, and the rest of the staff. We ate them with buttermilk biscuits split in half with hot Cracked-Pepper Gravy on top. With a big pot of strong coffee, it was one of the best breakfasts I ever had.

Cider Adobo

YIELD: 1 CUP

Adobo is a vinegary Mexican marinade. I turned it into a tangy sweet-and-sour sauce that tastes great on fried quail and can also be used as a glaze for grilled wild game.

$^3/_4$ cup red wine

$^3/_4$ cup apple cider vinegar

$^1/_4$ cup apricot preserves

$^1/_4$ cup honey

2 tablespoons packed brown sugar

1 teaspoon minced garlic

1 teaspoon peeled and minced fresh ginger

$^1/_2$ teaspoon kosher salt

1 scallion, thinly cut on the diagonal

$^1/_4$ cup chopped cilantro leaves

✪ Place all of the ingredients in a large, heavy pan and stir well to combine. ✪ Place the pan over medium-high heat and bring the mixture to a boil, watching carefully so it does not boil over. ✪ Reduce heat to medium and cook the adobo uncovered, stirring occasionally, until reduced by about 50 percent (to 1 cup). It will take 20 to 25 minutes to reduce. The consistency should be like syrup. ✪ Serve with the quail, or put the adobo into a jar to refrigerate for future use. ✪ Adobo will keep about 5 days in the refrigerator.

Cider Adobo

Bock-Battered Quail with Cider Adobo

YIELD: 4 SERVINGS

If you're not a hunter, you can buy frozen quail at a specialty butcher. Just make sure to buy the kind without any breading. To serve these fried quail for breakfast, just whip up some Buttermilk Biscuits (page 97) and substitute Cracked-Pepper Gravy (page 35) for the Cider Adobo.

BOCK BEER BATTER

1 cup club soda

1 cup Shiner Bock or any good bock beer

1 teaspoon kosher salt

Pinch of crushed red pepper flakes

$1^3/_4$ cups flour

4 semi-boned quail, cut into quarters

6 cups peanut oil

1 cup Cider Adobo (page 57)

✪ To prepare the beer batter, combine the soda, beer, salt, and red pepper flakes in a large, stainless steel bowl. ✪ Using a whisk, gradually add the flour, blending to avoid lumps. ✪ Stick your finger into the batter. If the batter is thick and sticks to your finger, it is ready. ✪ Add more flour if the batter seems thin.

✪ To prepare the quail, heat $2^1/_2$ to 3 inches of oil in a large, heavy skillet to 350° (when a drop of batter sizzles when dropped in the oil). ✪ A deep-fat fryer may also be used, but it will take more oil to fill. ✪ Dip each piece of quail into the batter, and slide it into the oil. ✪ Do as many pieces as possible without crowding or letting the temperature drop. ✪ Cook the quail about 8 to 10 minutes, turning once. ✪ Remove the quail to a paper towel–lined sheet pan to drain. ✪ Serve 4 pieces of quail, drizzled with the Cider Adobo, to each person.

Bock-Battered Quail with Cider Adobo

Stacked Pheasant Enchiladas in Salsa Verde

YIELD: 4 SERVINGS

Al used to raise pheasants on his ranch, and one year he had way too many, so we started serving them at the restaurant. Roasted pheasant always seems to come out too dry, so I decided to try putting them in enchiladas. Wow! What a difference. This is the best way to eat pheasant.

PHEASANT STUFFING

1 tablespoon olive oil

1 pound boneless and skinless
   pheasant meat

$^1/_2$ cup Red Chile Sauce
   (page 39)

Kosher salt to taste

Freshly ground pepper to taste

ENCHILADAS

$^1/_2$ cup vegetable oil

12 (8-inch) fresh corn tortillas

4 cups (about 1 pound) grated
   Monterey Jack

2 cups Salsa Verde (page 165)

4 heaping tablespoons sour cream

✪ To prepare the pheasant stuffing, heat the oil in a sauté pan, and add the pheasant meat. ✪ Sauté over medium heat, turning several times, until cooked through (about 6 minutes). ✪ Remove the pheasant from the heat and allow it to cool. ✪ Coarsely chop the meat into about 1-inch dice (you should have about 4 cups), and put it into a bowl. ✪ Add the chile, salt, and pepper, and mix thoroughly. ✪ Set aside.

✪ To prepare the enchiladas, just before serving time assemble all of the ingredients. ✪ Preheat the oven to 400°. ✪ Line a sheet pan with foil or lightly oil individual 10-inch ovenproof serving dishes. ✪ Set aside. ✪ Heat oil and prepare tortillas as described on page 42. Top the tortilla with $^1/_2$ cup pheasant mixture and $^1/_3$ cup cheese. Repeat this process for each serving, reserving $1^1/_3$ cups cheese for the top. The final tortilla will be topped only with cheese. Each serving will be a stack of three tortillas with pheasant between two layers and cheese on all three. Before adding the final cheese, cover each stack with $^1/_2$ cup salsa verde, spreading to cover the edges. Divide the cheese among the enchiladas. Bake them for 12 minutes, or until the sauce bubbles. Garnish each stack with a heaping tablespoon of sour cream. Serve at once.

Stacked Pheasant Enchiladas in Salsa Verde

Chuck Wagons

★ ★

A rancher named Charlie Goodnight is credited with inventing the chuck wagon in the 1870s to solve the problem of feeding cowboys in remote locations. When the trail-drive era ended and the cattle business became focused around the ranch house, chuck wagons became less common. They were still used at spring roundup, but by the 1920s, horse-drawn chuck wagons had been largely replaced by motorized versions.

On a few large Texas ranches, however, horse-drawn chuck wagons never disappeared. The Long X and the 06 ranches in the Trans-Pecos and the Pitchfork Ranch near Guthrie have used horse-drawn chuck wagons continuously since the turn of the century. "We have an old chuck wagon that was once used on the XIT Ranch," Cliff Teinert of the Long X says. "We used it all the time, but it's a museum piece, a real historical artifact, so I put it away. About four years ago, I built this new chuck wagon."

All that's visible of the Long X's new chuck wagon is the spring seat, a wooden water barrel, and the doubletree poking out from under the canvas tent flies. The canvas coverings shade the food and the cook on hot days, and keep them dry when it rains. The back of the chuck wagon is the business end. To set up camp, the cook stretches his canvas, then lowers a fold-down tailgate table that is covered with zinc and serves as a work surface. Behind it are dozens of drawers, cubbyholes, and compartments that hold his smaller tools and ingredients. Twenty-five-pound sacks of flour, Dutch ovens, and other supplies ride inside the wagon.

The chuck wagon has undergone a revival in recent times. As part of the movement to preserve the heritage of the Old West, old chuck wagons are being restored and modern replicas are being built. "A lot of ranches that stopped using horse-drawn chuck wagons years ago have gone back to them now," Cliff Teinert says.

At cowboy gatherings around the state, these old and new chuck wagons are the center of attention during cowboy cooking contests. As a member of the Western Heritage Chuck Wagon Association, Cliff Teinert frequently serves as a cowboy cook-off judge.

Roasted Game Hens with Molasses Rub

YIELD: 4 SERVINGS

You can substitute half chickens for the game hens in this recipe if you like. Cheese and Bacon Grits (page 122) are nice on the side.

2 quarts water
6 tablespoons kosher salt
4 tablespoons whole black peppercorns
8 sprigs thyme
12 cloves garlic, minced
2 tablespoons sugar
4 whole game hens
2 tablespoons unsalted butter, softened
1 cup Molasses Rub (page 200)

✪ Prepare a brine by mixing the water with the salt, pepper, thyme, garlic, and sugar in a container large enough to hold the game hens. ✪ A 2-gallon zipper-top plastic bag works well. ✪ Rinse the game hens. Then submerge them in the brine. ✪ Set them aside in the refrigerator for at least 2 hours, or overnight.

✪ To roast the hens, preheat the oven to 350°. ✪ Remove the hens from the brine and pat them dry. ✪ Rub them all over with the softened butter, and place them in a roasting pan. ✪ Bake the hens for 45 minutes, basting them occasionally with pan juices. ✪ Test for doneness with a meat thermometer inserted into the thigh. ✪ It should register 160°. ✪ The hens should be golden brown. ✪ Remove the hens from the oven and set them aside to rest.

✪ Preheat the broiler. ✪ Pat Molasses Rub on the hens, packing well to form a coating. ✪ Place the hens under the broiler until the rub caramelizes and darkens, about 5 minutes. ✪ Remove and serve.

Roasted Game Hens

Bacon-Wrapped Shrimp with Onion Marmalade

Bacon-Wrapped Shrimp with Onion Marmalade

YIELD: 6 SERVINGS

Here's an old cocktail party snack your parents used to serve. At the Reata, we serve the crispy shrimp and onion relish on Polenta Stars (page 112).

12 shrimp (about 1 pound), peeled, with tails left on
12 thin slices smoked bacon
1^1/$_2$ cups Onion Marmalade (page 168)

✪ Prepare a grill. The temperature should be medium-high. ✪ Clean and de-vein the shrimp. ✪ Wrap bacon tightly around each shrimp. Preheat the oven to 500°. ✪ Place the shrimp on the grill and cook them for 5 minutes. ✪ Turn them over and cook an additional 5 minutes. The bacon should be browned and crisp. ✪ Make sure the shrimp do not catch on fire from the bacon drippings igniting. ✪ Remove the shrimp to a sheet pan and place them in the preheated oven to finish cooking for 4 minutes, or until the bacon is cooked. ✪ Serve two shrimp with ^{1}/$_4$ cup of marmalade per person as an appetizer.

Bacon-
Wrapped
Shrimp

Refrigerator-Smoked Trout

YIELD: 2 SERVINGS

These tender smoked trout make a nice supper alongside a salad and some Dutch Oven Potatoes with Dried Fruit (page 107). You can also remove the skin and bones and use the fillets on salads, with scrambled eggs for breakfast, or on top of a bagel.

2 whole trout, cleaned (about 14 ounces each)
2 tablespoons olive oil
8 teaspoons Reata Grill Blend (page 200)

✪ Prepare an outdoor smoker as described on page 31, or use a stove-top smoker, described on page 27. For the stove-top model, use 2 tablespoons of "smoke dust." ✪ Rinse the trout well and rub them with olive oil. ✪ Sprinkle the trout generously with the Reata Grill Blend. ✪ Place the trout in the outdoor smoker or on the rack in the smoker. ✪ Smoke for 7 minutes (in the indoor smoker) or 15–30 minutes in the outdoor setup, or until the fish are cooked through and the flesh is firm. ✪ Serve the trout whole as an entrée, or remove the skin and bones and use the fillets for smoked fish recipes.

Cornmeal-Crusted Oysters with Horseradish Sour Cream

YIELD: 4 SERVINGS

The Texas oyster houses down around Rockport sell their oysters already shucked, in pint or quart jars. They aren't as shiny and perfect as oysters fresh out of their shells, but they are great for frying. And to tell the truth, I like fried oysters like these better than oysters on the half shell.

16 fresh oysters, shelled
$^3/_4$ cup cornmeal
1 teaspoon kosher salt
$^1/_2$ cup peanut oil
2 cups Horseradish Sour Cream (page 30)

✪ Remove any pieces of shell from the oysters and set aside. ✪ Blend the cornmeal and salt on a plate. ✪ Heat the oil in a large, shallow skillet. ✪ When the oil is hot, dust each oyster in the cornmeal and place in the pan. ✪ Panfry quickly, turning the oysters once. Do not crowd the oysters and do not overcook them. ✪ Serve 4 oysters on a small plate, with a dollop of Horseradish Sour Cream in the middle as a dip.

Catfish Cakes

YIELD: 10 3-OUNCE CAKES

Catfish is about the easiest thing to catch in Texas rivers, and it was one of the most common fish in cowboy cooking. It's a little bland, which is why I like to turn it into something more exciting—like these spicy fish cakes.

3 tablespoons vegetable oil

2 pounds boneless, skinless catfish fillets, cut into 1-inch dice

$^1/_2$ cup finely chopped red onion

1 jalapeño pepper, stemmed, seeded, and minced

$^1/_4$ cup finely diced red bell pepper

2 teaspoons minced garlic

$^1/_2$ cup mayonnaise

$^1/_4$ cup thinly sliced chives

$^1/_2$ cup minced cilantro leaves

1 tablespoon Dijon mustard

$1^1/_2$ cups fresh or dried white bread crumbs

2 eggs, lightly beaten

1 teaspoon lime zest

Kosher salt to taste

Freshly ground pepper to taste

$1^1/_2$ cups peanut oil

$^1/_2$ cup flour

✪ Heat the oil in a skillet over medium heat. ✪ Add the catfish, onion, peppers, and garlic. ✪ Sauté until the vegetables are wilted and the catfish is cooked through, about 5 minutes. ✪ In a large bowl, combine the cooked fish and vegetables, mayonnaise, chives, cilantro, mustard, crumbs, egg, zest, salt, and pepper. ✪ Form the mixed ingredients into 10 3-ounce patties. ✪ Pack the mixture fairly tight so it will stay together while cooking. ✪ Set aside on a plate.

✪ Heat the peanut oil in a pan until smoking slightly. ✪ Dust each cake with flour and gently slip it into the hot oil. ✪ Fry the cakes for approximately 2 minutes on each side, or until they are golden brown. Do not crowd the cakes; it is better to cook in batches. ✪ Remove the cakes and drain them on a paper towel–lined pan. Serve hot.

Catfish Cakes

Catfish Cakes

4

Dutch Ovens and One-Pot Meals

THE FIRST TIME I HAD TO COOK for a big outdoor picnic at the Post, I knew I was in for an education. Smoking meat outdoors was easy enough—I had a big smoker on a trailer rig for that—but I had no idea what else to cook. Shirley Rooney, who baked our bread and desserts at the time, told me to cook everything else in Dutch ovens. I confessed to Shirley that I had only a very vague notion of what a Dutch oven was and no idea of how to cook in one. So Shirley called a couple of old cowboys to come and help me out.

The Post is a historic fort and watering hole where all the big outdoor gatherings are held. When I got there on the morning of the party, these two old characters named Guy Lee and Tom Glasscock were already there, sitting beside their cook fires with their Dutch ovens bubbling away. They had set up and started cooking while it was still dark.

Watching Guy and Tom cook beans, fry potatoes, and simmer stew in their Dutch ovens taught me a lot in a very short time. It also answered some questions I always had about cowboy cooking. When you think of cooking on a campfire, a grill is the first thing that comes to mind. I always wondered why cowboy cooking included so many stews and simmered dishes.

Guy explained that if you have to use up a whole steer, you don't get to do much grilling. There's a lot of meat, but not much of it is steak. Tough cuts require long cooking, which is why chilis, stews, and braised meats were always the most common dishes in chuck wagon cooking. Besides, simmering a one-pot dish over a low fire is a pretty foolproof way to cook. And the Dutch oven made that style of cooking possible.

Dutch ovens were unknown in Mexico. They first arrived in Texas with the Anglos. At first, the *cocineros* used them to simmer beans and stews just like they did in the Mexican clay pots called *cazuelas*. But the Dutch oven could also be used to fry bacon and bake bread, so it made new kinds of cooking possible.

As the cattle business spread further away from the Mexican border—into Colorado, Nebraska, and Montana—black cooks, Irish cooks, and even some southern European cooks started working in the cowboy camps. They added gumbos, chicken and dumplings, Irish stews, braised pot roasts, and other dishes to the cowboy cooking style.

After working all morning on that party at The Post, I was getting pretty hungry, and I noticed Guy and Tom were eating something from one of their Dutch ovens. It looked like stew, and they offered to make me up a plate. It was delicious: I sopped up the gravy with some flour tortillas and asked for seconds. While they were spooning up my second helping, I asked them what I was eating.

"Son-of-a-bitch," said Guy with a sly grin. They didn't tell me what was in it until I was done with my second plate. Son-of-a-bitch is an old cowboy stew made out of calf's innards. It's one of those food names, like calf fries, that's supposed to confuse you about what you're really eating. But I guess if they called it calf innard stew, they would have had a hard time getting anybody to eat it for the first time. I know I would have passed.

Son-of-a-bitch is the most famous Dutch oven dish and a real favorite of cowboy cooks, probably because it gives them a great excuse to sit beside the fire for hours tending the pot and shooting the bull. Most cowboys love the stuff too, even if they were tricked into eating their first bowl.

At Reata, we serve a lot of Dutch oven stews and braised meats for lunch during the winter. Of course, we don't cook them in real cast-iron Dutch ovens at the restaurant—we use big stew pots. But while the cooking equipment may have changed, the one-pot meals that became a part of cowboy cooking thanks to Dutch ovens are still as popular as ever.

> Son-of-a-bitch is the most famous Dutch oven dish and a real favorite of cowboy cooks, probably because it gives them a great excuse to sit beside the fire for hours tending the pot and shooting the bull.

Jalapeño Beef Stew

YIELD: 4 SERVINGS

This sounds spicier than it really is; once the jalapeños are cooked, they mellow out and give this stew a nice pepper flavor, without a lot of burn. If you want to dress this up, you can top each bowl of stew with two Polenta Stars (page 112).

6 shallots, peeled

1 tablespoon olive oil

5 tablespoons unsalted butter

1 pound beef chuck, cut into
   1-inch squares

$1/_3$ cup flour

4 jalapeño peppers, stemmed and seeded

2 carrots, peeled and cut into
   2-inch rounds

1 large potato, peeled and cut into
   2-inch pieces

$1/_2$ red onion, peeled and diced

1 cup port

2 cups beef stock (fresh or canned)

1 tablespoon dried sage leaves

1 tablespoon dried oregano leaves

Kosher salt to taste

Freshly ground pepper to taste

Jalapeño Beef Stew cont.

✪ Preheat the oven to 350°. Toss the shallots with the olive oil, place them in a small pan, and roast them in the oven for 35 minutes, or until they are soft and brown. ✪ Heat the butter in a large, deep saucepan (that has a cover) over medium heat. ✪ While the butter is melting, toss the beef cubes with the flour to coat. ✪ Place the beef in the hot butter, increase the heat, and sauté the beef cubes on all sides for 5 minutes for rare and longer for medium or well done. Do not crowd the meat or it will steam rather than brown. ✪ Remove the pan from the heat, transfer the meat to a bowl, cover it loosely with foil to keep it warm, and set it aside.

✪ Mince the jalapeños. ✪ The peppers vary in heat, so the amount of peppers may be adjusted accordingly. ✪ Place the pan back over medium heat, and, in the remaining butter, sauté the peppers, carrots, potato, and onion, tossing to prevent burning until onions turn translucent. ✪ Add the wine, stock, sage, and oregano, gently stirring on the bottom of the pan to release any solidified pan juices. ✪ Cook the stew over low heat, with the lid slightly ajar, for 40 minutes. ✪ Add the reserved shallots and beef, stir to combine, and continue cooking for another 20 minutes. ✪ Test to see if the meat and vegetables are done. ✪ Season with salt and pepper.

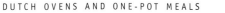

Pot Roast with Yams

YIELD: 6 TO 8 SERVINGS

The pointy-ended variety of sweet potatoes grown in East Texas is called a yam in Texas grocery stores, but you can use any kind of sweet potato with this pot roast. Serve with Yaller Bread with Pintos (page 98).

$^1/_2$ **cup flour**

1 teaspoon kosher salt

1 teaspoon Cracked Pepper (page 199)

4 to 6 pounds chuck roast

$^1/_2$ **cup corn oil**

$^3/_4$ **cup Ancho Ketchup (page 171)**

3 carrots, peeled and cut in 2 inch rounds

3 East Texas yams or sweet potatoes,
   cut into 2-inch pieces

1 onion, coarsely chopped

4 garlic cloves, minced

2 cups beef stock

✪ Season the flour with salt and pepper and blend thoroughly. Roll the roast in the flour-and-salt mixture. ✪ Heat the oil in an ovenproof stew pot large enough to cover the pot roast. Sear the roast for 4 minutes on each side, or until well browned. ✪ Add the ketchup, carrots, sweet potatoes, onion, and garlic. ✪ Cook the stew for 5 minutes. ✪ Add the beef stock, cover, and bring to a boil. ✪ Place the pan in a 300° oven and cook for $2^1/_2$ to 3 hours, or until the beef is very tender.

Braised Shanks

YIELD: 4 SERVINGS

Buffalo Osso Bucco is a very popular dish at Reata. I know that buffalo shanks are hard to find, so I used lamb shanks for this recipe. Lamb shanks are not only delicious—they are also usually inexpensive. Serve this with Garlic Mashed Potatoes (page 108).

1 tablespoon corn oil

4 lamb shanks (about 1 pound each)

Kosher salt to taste

Cracked Pepper to taste (page 199)

1 onion, chopped

5 cloves of garlic, coarsely chopped

5 tablespoons Red Chile Sauce (page 39)

$1^2/_3$ cups red wine

3 cups beef stock

4 sticks cinnamon

3 sprigs rosemary

$^1/_2$ cup butter, cold

✪ In a large stew pot, heat the oil over medium-high heat. Season the shanks with salt and pepper. ✪ Add the shanks, onion, and garlic to the oil, stirring to keep the onion and garlic from burning. Sear the shanks for 3 to 4 minutes on each side or until browned. ✪ When the shanks have been browned, add the chile sauce and cook for another 2 minutes. ✪ Add the red wine, beef stock, cinnamon, and rosemary. When this comes to a boil, lower the heat to simmer and cook the shanks covered for 3 hours, turning them occasionally. ✪ The meat should be extremely tender, but still attached to the bone. ✪ Remove the shanks and strain the cooking liquid. ✪ Reduce the cooking liquid over high heat by one quarter and whisk in the butter. Place one shank on each plate and pour some sauce over each.

Chicken Gumbo

YIELD: 12 SERVINGS

Some people say that gumbo without okra isn't authentic. But this is cowboy cooking, and since chuck wagons never had any okra either, you might say this gumbo is authentically inauthentic. I like to serve this over Green Mashed Potatoes (page 109).

10 tablespoons unsalted butter

$^2/_3$ cup flour

2 cups diced red bell pepper

2 cups diced green bell pepper

3 cups diced onion

2 stalks celery, diced

2 (15-ounce) cans diced tomatoes

5 tablespoons Worcestershire sauce

2 tablespoons Tabasco sauce

2 tablespoons tomato paste

1 bay leaf

2 teaspoons dried thyme leaves

2 teaspoons dried oregano leaves

1 teaspoon ground cayenne pepper

1 teaspoon ground white pepper

6 cups chicken stock

Meat from two whole cooked chickens, diced or pulled off the bone

Kosher salt to taste

Freshly ground pepper to taste

✪ Use a large, heavy pan that will hold at least 4 quarts. Melt the butter in the pan over medium heat. ✪ Stir in the flour, and cook over medium-low heat for about 20 minutes (or longer). The roux needs to become a rich brown color, without burning. Continual stirring with a wooden spoon is necessary. This step is what gives the gumbo its color and flavor. ✪ When the roux is the desired color, add the peppers, onion, and celery, sautéing until the vegetables are wilted, about 10 minutes. ✪ Next add the tomatoes, Worcestershire, Tabasco, tomato paste, bay leaf, thyme, oregano, cayenne, and white pepper. ✪ Stir to blend these ingredients. ✪ Whisk in the chicken stock, and cook the gumbo over medium heat for 30 minutes. ✪ Add the chicken meat and continue cooking for another 30 minutes. Season with salt and pepper. The gumbo should be fairly thick at serving time. ✪ Continue cooking to reduce if necessary. ✪ Serve at once over rice or mashed potatoes.

Chicken Gumbo

Chicken Gumbo

Son-of-a-Bitch

YIELD: 8 SERVINGS

This is Cliff Teinert's recipe for Son-of-a-Bitch, the most famous dish in cowboy cooking. "I don't think many people are going to cook it because you can't get some of the ingredients very easily," Cliff said. "But you ought to put it in your cookbook anyway. It's a good conversation piece."

Cliff explains that the dish also goes by more polite names, including Son-of-a-Gun, S.O.B., and Gentleman from Odessa. Why "Gentleman from Odessa?" I asked.

"Because anywhere else a gentleman from Odessa would be called a son-of-a-bitch," he laughed.

FROM A SUCKING CALF USE
The tongue
The marrow guts
$^1/_2$ the liver
The heart
1 kidney
The skirt steaks
The brains

1 large onion, chopped
2 cloves garlic, minced
Salt and pepper to taste

✪ Boil the tongue to remove the outer skin. ✪ Chop all the meats, vegetables, and innards, except the brains, into $^1/_2$-inch cubes and place in a large stewpot. Cover with water to 2 inches above the meat. ✪ Simmer for 2 hours until good and tender, adding more water as needed ✪ Thicken with the brains 15 minutes before serving. ✪ Serve with sourdough biscuits.

Son-of-a-Bitch

Sissified Son-of-a-Bitch

YIELD: 8 SERVINGS

Here's an adaptation of S.O.B. for the faint-hearted. It's basically a quick-cooking sweetbread-and-ribeye stew. The dish is simple to cook and the ingredients are pretty easy to find. It tastes great with Sourdough Biscuits (page 95).

1 pound veal sweetbreads

1 tablespoon kosher salt

1 tablespoon Cracked Pepper (page 199)

$1/_2$ cup flour

1 pound ribeye, cut into $1^1/_2$-inch cubes

2 tablespoons vegetable oil

1 onion, chopped

$1^1/_2$ cups beef stock

$1/_2$ cup red wine

$1/_2$ teaspoon dried thyme

1 large potato, peeled and cut into
    $1^1/_2$- inch cubes

✪ Blanch the sweetbreads in boiling water for 2 minutes. Remove all membranes. ✪ Set the sweetbreads on a piece of wax paper on a baking pan. Set another piece of wax paper and another baking pan on top of them and weigh them down with a 5-pound weight. ✪ Place the sweetbreads in the refrigerator for at least 2 hours, or overnight.

✪ Cut the flattened sweetbreads into $1^1/_2$-inch-long pieces. Mix the salt, pepper, and flour together in a shallow bowl. ✪ Dredge the ribeye and sweetbreads in the flour mixture. ✪ Heat the oil in a skillet. Sauté the ribeye, sweetbreads, and onions until they are well browned. ✪ Remove the ribeye and sweetbread from the pan and set aside. ✪ Add the stock, red wine, and thyme to the onions and bring to a boil. ✪ Add the potato and reduce the heat to a simmer. ✪ Cook for 20 minutes, or until the potato is tender. Add the sweetbreads and ribeye and cook over medium-high heat for 15 minutes, or until meat is cooked through. ✪ Serve hot in bowls.

Ranch Beans

Ranch Beans

YIELD: 10 SERVINGS

People like their beans without a lot of frills in West Texas. Serve these with Cow Town Coleslaw (page 142) and Yaller Bread with Pintos (page 98) for a cowboy version of a health-food lunch.

4 cups dried pinto beans

4 cups minced yellow onions plus

   $1^1/_2$ cups diced

$^1/_2$ cup pure chile powder

$^1/_4$ cup kosher salt

$^1/_2$ bunch cilantro, stemmed and chopped

4 tablespoons olive oil

2 cups diced red bell pepper

2 cups diced green bell pepper

✪ Wash the beans and sort through them to remove any foreign particles and broken beans. In a stockpot, cover the beans with cold water by 6 inches and soak them 6 hours, or overnight. ✪ Be sure the beans remain covered with water during the soaking process. ✪ Drain the beans and return them to the same pan. Cover them with fresh water by $1^1/_2$ inches. ✪ Add the minced onions, chile powder, salt, and cilantro and stir to blend. ✪ Bring the beans to a boil over medium heat. Reduce heat, cover, and cook until the beans are tender, about $2^1/_2$ hours. From time to time check and stir the beans. If necessary, add water as needed. Near the end of the cooking time the liquid should be almost absorbed. ✪ Close to serving time, heat the olive oil in a large sauté pan. ✪ When the oil is very hot, add the diced onion and peppers and cook them quickly, about 6 minutes, stirring and tossing, until crisp but tender. ✪ Stir this mixture into the beans. ✪ Serve at once.

Lamb Stew with Fancy Mushrooms

YIELD: 4 SERVINGS

Texas is one of the largest lamb-producing states in the country, but cowboys seldom eat lamb. Cattlemen and sheep ranchers never got along; they were always arguing over grazing rights. This mushroom and lamb stew probably could have ended the feud a long time ago.

$^1/_2$ cup flour

1 tablespoon Cracked Pepper (page 199)

1 tablespoon kosher salt

6 tablespoons unsalted butter

2 pounds leg of lamb, cut into 2 inch cubes

2 cups diced onion

8 cloves garlic, minced

$^1/_2$ cup red wine

$^1/_2$ cup beef stock

2 teaspoons fresh thyme leaves

1 pound fancy mushrooms (any combination of portobello, chanterelles, hedgehogs, or shiitakes), cleaned

1 tomato, chopped

Kosher salt to taste

Freshly ground black pepper to taste

1 avocado, cut into 8 slices, for garnish

✪ Preheat the oven to 300°. Mix the flour with the salt and pepper. Heat the butter in an ovenproof stew pot. ✪ Dredge the meat in the seasoned flour. ✪ When the butter is melted, add the meat to the stew pot along with the onions and garlic. Cook over high heat, stirring until well browned, about 7 to 10 minutes. ✪ Pour in the wine and beef stock and add the thyme. Bring the stew to a boil. Adjust heat to simmer and cook for 4 minutes. ✪ Remove from heat. ✪ Cover the pot and place it in the oven. After 10 minutes, remove the stew from oven and stir it well to incorporate the browned flour on the bottom of the pan. ✪ Return the pot to the oven and bake 20 minutes.

✪ If you are using portobello mushrooms, cut them into long $^1/_2$-inch-thick strips. Leave the other mushrooms whole.

✪ Remove the stew pot from the oven and place it on a burner over medium heat. ✪ Add the mushrooms and tomatoes and cook the stew for 10 minutes, or until the mushrooms are tender. ✪ Season with salt and pepper to taste. ✪ Spoon the stew into bowls and garnish each bowl with 2 avocado slices.

Lamb Stew

Dutch Ovens

★ ★

The three-footed, cast-iron pot with a concave lid got its name from the Dutch ped-dlers of the East Coast who introduced them to this country. Dutch ovens are the most versatile pot for outdoor cooking because you can use the same pots to fry, bake, or simmer. Dutch ovens come in diame-ters of eight, ten, twelve, fourteen, and sixteen inches, and most cooks choose one size that fits the number of people they usu-ally cook for.

"The trick to using a Dutch oven is handling the pot hook," an old cowboy cook told Robb and me while he was giving us a demonstration. A pot hook is a metal rod with a hook on the bottom. It's designed to lift the lid of the Dutch oven without burning your hands. The dish-shaped lid of a Dutch oven is designed to hold hot coals—with heat coming from both above and below. The food in the pot cooks evenly—but the lid is on a swivel handle and if the coals and ashes on top of it are not evenly bal-anced, it will tip to one side and dump the coals into the food.

"The lid still gets away from me every now and then," the cook confessed, "and any cowboy cook who says it's never happened to him is a damn liar." When you start out a new oven, the cook advised, just wipe it with a dry rag to clean it, never use soap and water. Grease it heavily with Crisco in between uses. If you're going to put the Dutch oven away for a while, use olive oil—it doesn't go rancid. The bottom of a Dutch oven should be as slick as glass.

You can buy Dutch ovens at most camping outfitters or order them by mail from Big Bend Saddlery, P.O. box 38, Alpine, Texas 79831, 800-634-4502.

5

Sourdough, Biscuits, and
Yaller Breads

IF YOU'VE EVER READ LARRY McMURTRY'S *Lonesome Dove*, you may remember what a big deal Gus McRae made out of making biscuits. Gus wasn't the only cowboy who was something of a fanatic when it came to baking. Old-time cowboys would put up with a lot of greasy chili and watery beans, as long as there was some decent bread to be had. Great cowboy cooks, or "doughpunchers," as they are often called, have always been judged first and foremost by their baking.

Baking is not usually any great test of cooking skills, but baking bread and biscuits was a real challenge in the Old West. After all, chuck wagons don't have ovens. The baking had to be done in a Dutch oven over a campfire. If you've never tried this style of baking, let me tell you—it's tricky.

If baking in a Dutch oven wasn't hard enough, to complicate things further, there wasn't any yeast around either. Every cowboy cook had an earthenware crock of sourdough starter, and he took care of it like it was his best friend. The natural yeasts in sourdough will die if they get too cold. On cold days, the crock had to be kept close to the cooking fire and on cold nights, many a cowboy cook cuddled up with his sourdough to keep it alive.

We take great pride in keeping the western bread- and biscuit-baking traditions alive at the Reata. We always bake our sourdough biscuits and breads fresh from scratch at every meal. Once you get a starter going, you'll be amazed at how easy it is.

Sourdough Starter

YIELD: 3 CUPS

You can buy a powdered sourdough starter at a specialty food store and follow the directions if you want. Or you can follow this recipe and make one from scratch the way the old doughpunchers did. Be sure to give your sourdough starter a name. Ours is called "chico."

2 cups flour
1$^1/_2$ cups water
2 tablespoons plain yogurt
$^1/_2$ teaspoon malted milk

✪ Combine all of the ingredients in a mixer fitted with the paddle attachment. Blend on low speed for 3 minutes. ✪ Pour the mixture into a container and cover it loosely with plastic wrap. ✪ Let the starter sit at room temperature for several days before using, stirring it every couple of days. ✪ Each time you use some starter you must "feed" the original mixture with a new mixture equal to the amount used. Putting the mixture in the refrigerator will stop the development of the starter. If you will not use it for long periods of time, store it in the refrigerator and take it back out to redevelop before use. ✪ The mixture should have a sour smell. The recipe may be doubled for the first time. Then make smaller batches later to feed the original.

Sourdough Onion Flatbread

YIELD: 11 FLATBREADS

Mexican cooks didn't cut their sourdough into biscuit rounds, they baked it flat and cut it into wedges. They called the disc-shaped loaves "sourdough pan." The Mexican pronunciation has a bit of a G sound on the end, like "pahng."

8 cups bread flour

4 teaspoons kosher salt plus 4 teaspoons
  for sprinkling

6 tablespoons dry yeast

9 cloves garlic, minced

1$^1/_4$ cups minced scallions (about 1 bunch)

$^3/_4$ cup minced red onion (about $^1/_2$ onion)

1 cup Sourdough Starter (page 89)

3 tablespoons olive oil plus 4 tablespoons
  to brush on dough

2 to 3 cups warm water

✪ Use at least a 5-quart mixing bowl and a mixer with a paddle and dough hook for this recipe. ✪ Place all of the ingredients in the mixing bowl, except the water, in the order given. ✪ Blend all of the ingredients, using the paddle attachment, with the mixer at medium-low speed. Begin slowly adding the water, letting it absorb before adding more. ✪ As the water is absorbed and the dough comes together, stop the machine and change to the dough hook. ✪ Check the dough at this time. It needs to be soft, not dry and crumbly or wet and sticky. ✪ Continue adding water if necessary. The amount of water will vary depending on the flour and the weather. ✪ When the appropriate consistency is reached, turn the mixer speed to low and mix the dough for approximately 15 minutes, or until the dough forms a ball around the top of the hook. The dough should be smooth and very tight.

✪ Lightly oil a large bowl. ✪ Pull the dough from the hook. ✪ Place it on a smooth, lightly floured surface, knead it 5 times, and set it in the oiled bowl. Turn the dough once to oil all sides. ✪ Cover the dough loosely with plastic wrap, and set it aside in a warm, draft-free area to proof. The dough should double in bulk in 30 to 45 minutes.

✪ After the dough has risen, punch it down, and turn it out onto a lightly floured smooth surface. ✪ Knead the dough several times, rotating it as you go. ✪ Portion the dough into 6-ounce balls (for 11 balls total, if you don't have a scale). ✪ Let the dough rest for a few minutes. ✪ Meanwhile, lightly oil 2 sheet pans (or use parchment paper). Take each dough ball and flatten it to 5 inches across and set it on the prepared pan. ✪ Brush the tops with the additional olive oil and sprinkle with salt. Set the dough aside again in a warm place to let rise until doubled in bulk and about $1^1/_2$ -inches thick. This should take anywhere from 20 to 40 minutes. ✪ During this time, preheat the oven to 375°. ✪ Place the bread in the oven and bake for 15 minutes, or until the tops are golden brown.

Sourdough Onion Flatbread

Sourdough Pancakes

YIELD: 36 PANCAKES

Flapjacks, splatter dabs, whatever you call them, sourdough pancakes are the best kind. Try these with real maple syrup and crispy bacon.

4 cups bread flour

$^1/_4$ cup sugar

2 teaspoons kosher salt

2 tablespoons baking powder

4 eggs

3 cups milk

8 tablespoons unsalted butter, melted

$1^1/_2$ cups sourdough starter (page 89)

2 teaspoons pure vanilla extract

✪ In a large bowl, sift or combine all of the dry ingredients together. In another bowl, beat the eggs with a whisk. ✪ Add the milk, butter, sourdough starter, and vanilla to the eggs. Blend to combine. ✪ Add the liquid ingredients to the dry ingredients, blending with a whisk. ✪ Do not overwork the mixture. ✪ Heat a lightly oiled or buttered nonstick flat griddle to medium-high. ✪ When the griddle is hot, ladle one quarter cup of batter onto the griddle and cook for 3 minutes on each side, or until golden brown. Remove finished pancakes to a serving plate and keep warm, covered, in a 200° oven until serving time. ✪ Repeat cooking process until batter is finished.

Sourdough Pancakes

Sourdough Biscuits

Sourdough Biscuits

Cowboys called sourdough rolls "biscuits." The difference between biscuits and rolls, nowadays, is that biscuits are usually made with baking soda and rolls are made with yeast. But commercial baking soda didn't come along until late in the cowboy era, so back then there was no such difference.

2 cups flour

2 teaspoons baking powder

$^1/_2$ teaspoon baking soda

1 teaspoon salt

2 tablespoons sugar

$^1/_2$ cup unsalted butter, chilled

$^3/_4$ cup sourdough starter (page 89)

✪ Prepare a baking sheet with parchment paper, or lightly coat it with butter. Set aside. ✪ Combine the flour, baking powder, soda, salt, and sugar in a large bowl. ✪ Cut the butter into small pieces and work it into the dough with a pastry cutter, a fork, or your hands. ✪ There should be tiny pieces of butter evenly distributed throughout the dry ingredients. ✪ Add the sourdough starter and stir to blend until the flour is almost absorbed. ✪ Turn the dough out onto a lightly floured surface and knead several times until it is smooth. Do not overwork the dough. This dough should be soft but not sticky or too dry. Roll the dough to a thickness of $^3/_4$- to 1-inch thick. ✪ Cut 2-inch rounds out of the dough with a biscuit cutter and place them on the prepared pan. ✪ Make the cuts as close as possible to each other. Reroll the remaining scraps and cut again. ✪ Let the biscuits rise at room temperature until doubled in size, 10 to 30 minutes. ✪ Preheat the oven to 400°. ✪ Bake the biscuits in the oven for 12 to 15 minutes. ✪ Remove from oven and serve hot.

Cowboy Sourdough Baking

★ ★ ★ ★ ★ ★ ★ ★ ★ ★ ★ ★ ★ ★ ★ ★ ★ ★ ★ ★

Dressed in a Stetson, jeans, and boots, with a red bandana around his neck, Brad Whitfield looks a little out of place with flour all over his hands. He has just come from his other ranch chores, but now he's rolling out a batch of dough. "I mixed some of this sourdough starter with flour and sugar an hour ago," he says pointing a floury finger at a five-gallon earthenware crock tucked into a cubbyhole on the working end of the chuck

wagon. "And I put some baking soda in too, just for insurance. I never measure anything—it comes out different every time." Brad uses an empty can with both ends missing as a cutter. After heavily oiling the bottom of the Dutch oven, he begins to lay the rolls in, packing them tightly together.

"Six or seven years ago, I started entering chuck-wagon cooking competitions," Brad says. "I was just in it for the beer drinking, but I won the bread-baking competition in Fort Worth, Lubbock, Midland, and I don't remember where else. Now I'm stuck cooking all the time. I'd rather be out punching cows."

After the rolls have risen, Brad heads for the campfire with a flat shovel and comes back with a load of hot coals. He dumps the coals on the bare ground and sets the Dutch oven on top of them. Then he goes back for another load of coals. This time he sets the coals on top of the Dutch oven's concave lid. The idea is to bake the bread with even heat from above and below. After fifteen minutes, Brad moves the Dutch oven off the coals.

"The bottom's pretty brown by now," he says. The most common problem of Dutch-oven baking is burning the bottom of the bread, he explains. Since the rolls are sitting right on the cast iron, they receive more heat from the bottom than the top. The trick is to move the Dutch oven off the coals and continue baking using only the coals on the lid. After another ten minutes, the smell of fresh-baked bread begins to fill the air.

"When you smell that yeasty bread smell, they're just starting to brown on top," Brad says. He carefully lifts the lid with his pothook and checks them, but they are still pale. "Got to turn the heat up a little," Brad says. He takes off his cowboy hat and fans the coals until they glow bright red. After another minute or two, he sets the lid aside and offers everybody one of his award-winning sourdough biscuits. They are a little crusty on the outside and meltingly tender inside, with the sharp tang of sourdough. "They don't even need butter, do they?" he asks through a smile and a mouthful of sourdough.

Buttermilk Biscuits

YIELD: 20 BISCUITS

Biscuits are served with breakfast, lunch, and dinner in West Texas, but they've got to be fresh from the oven. Save your leftover biscuits for Biscuit Pudding with Southern Comfort Sauce (page 180).

$3^1/_2$ cups flour

5 teaspoons baking powder

$1^1/_2$ teaspoons baking soda

2 tablespoons sugar

1 teaspoon salt

$1^1/_2$ cups chopped pecans (optional)

$^1/_2$ cup shortening

$^1/_4$ cup unsalted butter

$1^1/_2$ cups buttermilk

✪ Preheat the oven to 400°. ✪ Prepare a baking sheet with parchment paper, or lightly coat it with butter. Set aside. ✪ Combine the flour, baking powder, soda, sugar, and salt in a large bowl. ✪ Add the pecans if you're using them. ✪ Blend the dry ingredients with a whisk. Add the shortening and butter and work them in using a pastry cutter, fork, or your hands. ✪ Pour in the buttermilk and mix the dough until most of the flour is absorbed. ✪ Turn the dough out onto a lightly floured surface and knead it 4 to 6 times. You should have a stiff dough that is not sticky. ✪ Roll the dough to a thickness of 1 to $1^1/_2$ inches. ✪ Cut $2^1/_2$-inch rounds out of the dough with a biscuit cutter and place them on the prepared pan. ✪ Reroll the remaining scraps and cut again. ✪ Let the biscuits rise at room temperature until doubled in size, 10 to 30 minutes. The tops may be brushed with melted butter for a browner top. ✪ Bake the biscuits in the oven for 12 to 15 minutes. ✪ Remove from the oven and serve hot.

Yaller Bread with Pintos

YIELD: 8 LARGE SQUARES

Cornbread, also known as corn pone, johnnycake, and yaller bread, was always more common than sourdough down in South Texas. Cowboys there liked to eat their yaller bread with molasses and frijoles. This one already has the frijoles in it.

$1^1/_2$ cups buttermilk

3 eggs, lightly beaten

3 tablespoons sugar

1 teaspoon baking soda

$^1/_2$ cup Ranch Beans (page 83)

$^1/_2$ cup fresh corn kernels

1 cup flour

$1^1/_2$ cups fine yellow cornmeal

$^1/_2$ cup unsalted butter, melted

✪ Preheat the oven to 375°. Prepare an 8 by 8-inch pan or cast-iron skillet by rubbing with oil or melted butter. Set aside. ✪ Combine the buttermilk, eggs, sugar, and soda and mix well. ✪ Add the beans and the corn. ✪ Sift together the flour and cornmeal. ✪ Slowly add the flour mixture to the liquids, whisking until well incorporated. ✪ Whisk in the melted butter. ✪ Pour the batter into pan or cast-iron skillet and bake for 40 minutes, or until a toothpick comes out clean.

Yaller Bread

Yaller Bread with Pintos

Cornbread Dressing

YIELD: 6 TO 9 SERVINGS

We started making this dressing at Reata to use up our leftover corn bread. You can serve it with roasted pork as a spicy side dish, or with your turkey on Thanksgiving.

4 cups crumbled Yaller Bread with Pintos
  (page 98)
2 jalapeño peppers, stemmed and seeded
6 tablespoons unsalted butter
2 cups diced yellow onion
1 cup diced celery
2 cloves garlic, minced
$^1/_3$ cup chopped pecans (optional)
1 teaspoon dried thyme leaves
Kosher salt to taste
Freshly ground pepper to taste
3 eggs, lightly beaten
1 to 1$^1/_4$ cups chicken stock

✪ Put the crumbled cornbread into a large bowl. ✪ Preheat the oven to 325°. Butter an 8 by 8-inch pan and set aside. ✪ Mince the jalapeños and set aside. ✪ In a large, heavy skillet, heat the butter over medium heat. ✪ Add the jalapeños, onions, celery, and garlic and sauté, stirring constantly, until the vegetables have softened. ✪ Add the pecans if you're using them and thyme, season with salt and pepper. ✪ Spoon this mixture over the cornbread and toss lightly with a large spoon. ✪ Add the eggs and toss to blend. ✪ Add half the chicken stock and stir until the mixture is very moist, but short of soupy. ✪ Add the remainder as needed to maintain this consistency. Spoon the dressing into the prepared pan. ✪ Bake the dressing for 30 to 40 minutes, or until it sets and the top is lightly browned. ✪ Cut and serve hot.

Chorizo and Garlic Bread Pudding

YIELD: 4 TO 6 SERVINGS

Savory bread puddings make an unusual but tasty side dish. The sausage in this bread pudding makes it hearty enough to turn a plate of vegetables into a good dinner.

1 tablespoon unsalted butter

1 tablespoon diced red onion

1 tablespoon minced garlic

$^3/_4$ pound Chihuahuan Chorizo (page 48)

1 teaspoon dried oregano leaves

1 cup heavy cream

2 eggs

3 cups cubed Sourdough Onion Flatbread
   (page 90)

1 cup grated Parmesan or Asiago cheese

Kosher salt to taste

Freshly ground pepper to taste

✪ In a skillet large enough to hold all of the ingredients, melt the butter. Add the onion, garlic, chorizo, and oregano. ✪ Sauté over medium heat until the meat is cooked, about 5 minutes. ✪ Add the cream and stir well. Remove the pan from the heat. ✪ Whisk the eggs and blend them into the cream and meat. ✪ Add the bread, cheese, salt, and pepper; blend well and let mixture sit for 20 minutes. ✪ Meanwhile, preheat the oven to 375° and butter an 8 by 8-inch square or oval baking dish. ✪ Blend the bread mixture again and pour into the prepared pan. ✪ Bake in the oven for 25 minutes. ✪ Cut into squares and serve warm.

Chorizo and Garlic
Bread Pudding

6

Potatoes, Vegetables, and Other Touchy Subjects

Bick's first blow struck him squarely in the jaw but Jett Rink's
monolithic head scarcely went back with it...
"My, you're techy, Bick," he said. "You're techy as a cook."

—Edna Ferber, *Giant*

COWBOY COOKS HAVE ALWAYS BEEN "TECHY," mainly because nobody wanted the job. In some small outfits, one of the cowboys was picked to be the cook, usually the oldest, weakest, or most inept hand in the outfit. Of course that made the man ornery from the start. Nicknames like "belly-cheater," "biscuit shooter," "dough-puncher," "beanmaster," "grub-spoiler," and "pot-rassler" didn't help either.

But around the chuck wagon, the cook was king. Cowboys who got caught sneaking snacks, forgot to wash their dishes, came late to dinner, or, worst of all, complained about the food came to regret it. Rocks in your beans, dishwater for coffee, and pies filled with old coffee grounds and potato peelings were the sort of special treats you could expect from a cook who was sore at you.

There're a lot of old stories in western lore about touchy cooks. One chuck-wagon cook who had enough of his job took off in the middle of the night—after he filled the

cowboys' boots with molasses. Even the trail boss got it sometimes. When the head honcho of a northern Plains outfit showed up late for dinner one night and then had the nerve to complain that his food was cold, the cook beat him over the head with a skillet and a coffeepot.

Bobby McKnight, of the McKnight Ranch down by Marfa, told me about a fight between an ill-tempered cook and some cowboys that nearly ended in a gunfight, just ten years ago. "We had these cowboys back in the eighties that got into it with the cook one time," Bobby remembers. "They wanted him to make fried potatoes. He had some potatoes, but he refused to cook them. I don't remember why—said he was saving them or something. The cowboys told him he was just too lazy. They all started screaming at each other and throwing things. Next thing you know somebody pulled a gun. All over damned potatoes."

Potatoes have always been a touchy subject around the chuck wagon. Most cowboys loved potatoes and most chuck-wagon cooks hated them. Potatoes were heavier than beans; they often went bad; and they had to be peeled. Still, they were the closest thing to a vegetable some cowboys ever saw. I love potatoes myself, and I tend to serve them with just about everything. I'm always looking for new things to do with potatoes. I wish I could say I paid as much attention to other vegetables.

A lot of people assume that cowboys wouldn't eat vegetables, but that's not true. Cowboys knew that they'd get scurvy without any fruits or vegetables, so they ate all they could get—which wasn't much. It wasn't until canned goods reached the West that there was a steady supply of vegetables to be had. Canned corn and canned tomatoes were the first and most plentiful. The corn was used in cooking, and everybody liked it well enough. But it was the tomatoes that became near and dear to cowboys' hearts.

Cowboys carried canned tomatoes around in their saddlebags. They ate them as a snack and added them to their food, but it was the juice that they really loved. The water in many of the streams and rivers in West Texas is hard and bitter-tasting. Water from some rivers is so full of mineral salts you can barely drink it or cook in it. The soft tomato water was the sweetest-tasting liquid cowboys had to drink, and the acidity improved the flavor of their food.

Potatoes have always been a touchy subject around the chuck wagon. Most cowboys loved potatoes and most chuck-wagon cooks hated them.

Green beans came along after the chuck-wagon days, when the cattle business relocated to ranch headquarters. It was easy to grow green beans—all you had to do was throw a couple of dried pinto beans in a hole and water them. Then you picked the young green pods before the beans were full-grown. Tomatoes were grown in ranch house gardens too, but cowboys were never big on the fresh variety. They always preferred the kind that came in cans, with all that sweet tomato water.

When it comes to vegetables, I have to admit that I'm a little "techy" myself. I'm amazed by some of the things I see other chefs doing with vegetables. When I was learning how to cook out in the Trans-Pecos, it was hard enough to get iceberg lettuce on a regular basis—fresh asparagus was a once-a-year kind of treat. So I never got a chance to experiment much. As a result, the vegetables at Reata tend to be simple side dishes that go well with meat. Luckily, there aren't a lot of vegetarian cowboys, so we don't get too many complaints.

Dutch Oven Potatoes with Dried Fruit

Dutch Oven Potatoes with Dried Fruit

YIELD: 6 TO 8 SERVINGS

The sweet flavors of the dried fruit in this old-fashioned potato casserole go really well with roast pork or poultry.

2 pounds russet potatoes, scrubbed

$^1/_2$ cup grated Parmesan cheese

2 cups Dried Fruit Mix (see page 201)

2 cups heavy cream

Kosher salt to taste

Freshly ground black pepper to taste

3 tablespoons unsalted butter

✪ Preheat the oven to 300°. ✪ Use an 8 by 8-inch baking dish or one of similar size, and butter the bottom and sides with 1 tablespoon butter. Wash the potatoes and thinly slice them, using a mandolin, to approximately $^1/_{16}$ inch thick. If slicing by hand, make the slices paper thin. ✪ Layer one fifth of the sliced potatoes into the baking dish, making 2 thin layers of potatoes overlapping. ✪ Sprinkle with 2 teaspoons of the Parmesan cheese. Top with $^1/_2$ cup fruit, salt, pepper, and $^1/_2$ cup cream. ✪ Repeat this step 4 more times, ending with the potatoes. ✪ Top the potatoes with the remaining cream and the 3 tablespoons of the butter cut into small pieces. ✪ Sprinkle with the rest of the cheese.

✪ Cover the pan with foil and bake for 2 hours. Uncover the pan and bake for an additional 15 minutes to lightly brown the top. For a darker brown, place the potatoes under the broiler for a few minutes. ✪ Remove the potatoes from the oven and let them sit for 15 minutes before serving. ✪ Cut the potatoes into squares with a sharp knife.

Dutch Oven Potatoes

Garlic Mashed Potatoes

YIELD: 4 SERVINGS

The thick steak of my dreams always comes with mashed potatoes. Garlic mashed potatoes, horseradish mashed potatoes, scallion mashed potatoes— I love them all.

2 pounds russet potatoes
15 cloves garlic, peeled
5 tablespoons unsalted butter
$^3/_4$ cup heavy cream
Kosher salt to taste
Freshly ground pepper to taste

✪ Peel potatoes and cut them into $1^1/_2$-inch thick pieces. ✪ Place the pieces in a large, heavy saucepan, along with the garlic cloves, and cover the potatoes with 1 inch of cold water. ✪ Place the saucepan on high heat, and bring the water to a boil. ✪ Turn the heat down to medium, cover the pot, and cook the potatoes until they are just soft when tested with the tip of a knife, about 20 minutes.

✪ While the potatoes are cooking, heat the butter and cream in another saucepan. Reduce by one fourth.

✪ When potatoes and garlic are cooked, drain them. ✪ Mash the potatoes and garlic while pouring in the hot cream mixture. ✪ Stir the salt and pepper into the finished potatoes. ✪ Serve at once or place the covered bowl over another pan of simmering water to keep warm.

Variations

Blue Cheese Mashed Potatoes: Omit the garlic and fold a cup of blue cheese into the hot potatoes before serving.

Green Mashed Potatoes: Omit the garlic. Melt the butter in a saucepan. Combine the melted butter with 3 coarsely chopped scallions in the bowl of a food processor. Purée the scallions into a paste and add them to the cream. Proceed as directed.

Texas 1015s: The Sweetest Onions in the West

★ ★ ★ ★ ★ ★ ★ ★ ★ ★ ★ ★ ★ ★ ★ ★ ★ ★

Some of the best onion farms in Texas are located in Presidio, near the Rio Grande River just south of the Trans-Pecos. Every spring they bring in a huge crop of 1015 supersweet onions. A 1015 onion is the size of a softball and very juicy.

In national taste tests against Vidalia, Maui, and Walla Walla onions, the Texas 1015 has been judged the sweetest raw onion in the country. Developed by Dr. Leonard Pike, Professor of Horticulture at Texas A&M University, the Texas 1015 onion has become one of the state's major agricultural crops.

The strange name is a scientific designation that was used in the testing process. The story goes that several different plots of the onions were planted in an experiment to determine the ideal planting date. The 1015s (planted on October 15) did much better than the 1030s (planted on October 30). Dr. Pike wanted to market them as Texas SuperSweet onions, but by the time they were ready to sell, the onion farmers were so used to calling them 1015s that the name just stuck.

Each 1015 onion has a little sticker on it to prevent onion counterfeiting.

Buttermilk-Battered 1015 Onion Rings

Buttermilk-Battered 1015 Onion Rings

YIELD: 4 SERVINGS OR 28 RINGS

Texas 1015 onions make the best onion rings in the world. Not only are the onions very sweet, they are also gigantic, which makes for some pretty impressive onion rings. Serve these with Ancho Ketchup (page 171). If you can't find 1015's, sweet onions like Vidalias, Mauis, and Walla Wallas will also work well.

2 large 1015 onions

1$^1/_2$ cups Flour Spice (page 32)

4 eggs

1 cup buttermilk

1 cup Shiner Bock beer or
  any good bock beer

1 teaspoon salt

5 cups peanut oil

Kosher salt to taste

Freshly ground pepper to taste

✪ Cut the two ends off of the onions and discard. ✪ Slice the onions to produce rings about 1$^1/_2$ inches thick. ✪ Remove the very center of the onion and discard. ✪ Separate the rings and set aside. ✪ Put the flour spice in a bowl or on a plate and set it aside. ✪ Prepare the batter by whisking together the eggs, buttermilk, beer, and salt. ✪ Heat the oil in a heavy, deep saucepan or deep fat fryer to a temperature of 350° or until a drop of batter sizzles when dropped in it. ✪ When the correct temperature is reached, begin the breading process with the onion rings. ✪ Dip each ring into the batter, dredge it in the Flour Spice, place it back into the batter and again into the Flour Spice. The final dredging should evenly coat the batter so the rings are dry on the outside. ✪ Slide the prepared rings into the hot oil. ✪ Fry the rings for 4 to 6 minutes, maintaining an even temperature, until they are golden brown. ✪ Remove the rings with a skimmer or slotted spoon, as they become golden brown, to drain on a tray lined with paper towels. ✪ When all of the onion rings are cooked, stack them on a serving platter.

Polenta Stars

YIELD: 4 TO 6 SERVINGS

Polenta was actually very common in cowboy cooking, except they called it "cornmeal mush." You can call these "cornmeal mush stars" if you like. At Reata, we serve Bacon-Wrapped Shrimp (page 65) on one of these stars and top it with a spoonful of Onion Marmalade (page 168). You can also serve Polenta Stars instead of potatoes, or use them to dress up a bowl of stew.

1 tablespoon olive oil

1 cup minced shallots

$^3/_4$ cup minced red onion (about $^1/_2$ onion)

8 scallions, thinly sliced

3 cups water

3 cups milk

2 teaspoons dried thyme leaves

1 teaspoon kosher salt

1 teaspoon freshly ground pepper

$^1/_4$ cup unsalted butter

$1^1/_2$ cups quick cooking polenta

1 cup grated Asiago

✪ Heat the oil in a large, heavy, deep saucepan. ✪ Add the shallots, onion, and scallions, and sauté them over medium heat until they are wilted, about 5 minutes. ✪ Add the water, milk, thyme, salt, pepper, and butter. Bring the mixture to a boil. ✪ Adjust the heat to a simmer. Pour polenta in with one hand while whisking with the other to prevent any lumps from forming. ✪ When all of the polenta is whisked in, change to a long-handled wooden spoon and stir until polenta thickens and absorbs the liquid. Lower heat if necessary. The cooking time should range from 10 to 15 minutes. ✪ Remove the pan from the heat and stir the Asiago into the hot mixture. ✪ Butter a sheet pan and spread the polenta evenly into the pan, smoothing with a spatula. ✪ Cover the mixture with plastic and refrigerate. ✪ At serving time, cut the polenta into stars or other shapes. ✪ Heat the stars by pan sautéing, grilling, or baking in the oven. ✪ Serve hot.

Cow Camp Creamed Corn

YIELD: 6 SERVINGS

This stuff is nothing like the bland, disgusting, mushy creamed corn that comes in a can. The flavors of smoked bacon, peppers, and fresh cream make it an excellent side dish with grilled fish or chicken. We also serve it at Reata with Chicken Chile Rellenos (see page 45).

2 cups corn kernels (cut from about 2 ears)

4 slices smoked bacon, diced

$^3/_4$ cup diced red onion

1 clove garlic, minced

2 cups heavy cream

$^3/_4$ cup thinly sliced scallions (about 8 scallions)

$^3/_4$ cup diced red pepper (about 1 pepper)

Kosher salt to taste

Freshly ground black pepper to taste

✪ Preheat the oven to 350°. ✪ Sauté the diced bacon over medium heat, using an ovenproof skillet. ✪ As the bacon begins to crisp, add the onion and garlic and cook briefly. ✪ Add one cup of the corn kernels, stir well, and place the skillet in the 350° oven for 10 minutes to roast the corn. ✪ Remove from the oven and add the cream. ✪ Purée the mixture in a blender and return to a clean saucepan. ✪ Add the remaining corn, scallions, and red pepper. ✪ Place the saucepan over medium heat and simmer until the creamed corn is thickened and reduced to about 3 cups, stirring to prevent scorching. This will take about 20 minutes. ✪ Season with salt and pepper.

Creamed Spinach with Texas Tarragon

YIELD: 5 TO 6 SERVINGS

This rich creamed spinach is all you need to kickstart a slow dinner. Try it with some broiled lamb chops or a big, juicy steak. Texas tarragon, also known as Mexican mint marigold, is an herb that grows wild in some parts of Texas. It has the same sort of licorice aroma as tarragon.

$1^1/_2$ tablespoons unsalted butter

1 cup diced yellow onion

$1/_2$ teaspoon minced garlic

2 tablespoons fresh Texas tarragon,
   chopped, or 1 teaspoon dried tarragon

$1^1/_4$ cups heavy cream

$2/_3$ cup (about 2 ounces) grated Parmesan cheese

1 pound cleaned fresh spinach, stems
   removed and well drained

1 cup fine fresh or dried white bread crumbs

Kosher salt to taste

Freshly ground pepper to taste

✪ In a large, heavy saucepan heat the butter over medium heat. ✪ Add the onions and sauté until they are transparent. ✪ Add the garlic and sauté 4 minutes. ✪ Add the Texas tarragon and sauté another minute. ✪ Add the heavy cream, bring it to a simmer, and stir in the cheese. ✪ When the cheese has melted, add the spinach, bread crumbs, salt, and pepper. ✪ Stir to combine all of the ingredients. ✪ Cover the pan and let the spinach wilt for 4 minutes. ✪ Uncover the pan and cook the spinach an additional 6 minutes, stirring to blend the spinach and sauce. ✪ Serve at once.

Creamed Spinach

Char-Grilled Squash

YIELD: 4 SERVINGS

Grilling zucchini and summer squash gives them a great smoky, charred flavor. And if you've got the grill going for your main course anyway, it's really easy.

2 zucchini squash
2 yellow squash
2 tablespoons olive oil
Kosher salt to taste
Freshly ground black pepper to taste

✪ Wash and dry the squash. ✪ Cut the root ends off and slice the squash lengthwise in $\frac{1}{2}$-inch-thick slices. ✪ Lay the squash slices out on a plate and sprinkle them with oil, salt, and pepper. ✪ Place the slices on a very hot grill and cook on both sides until well done, about 10 minutes.

Asparagus with Mescal Hollandaise

YIELD: 4 SERVINGS

When I was a kid, my Dad loved canned asparagus with his steak. I never liked asparagus until I started cooking it fresh. Now I love asparagus with steaks myself—especially with hollandaise on top.

1¹/₂ pounds asparagus
3 tablespoons olive oil
Kosher salt to taste
Freshly ground pepper to taste
1 cup Mescal Hollandaise (recipe follows)

✪ Prepare the asparagus by removing the tough root end. If asparagus is thick, the stalks may be peeled. ✪ Bring a large pot of salted water to a boil. ✪ Drop the asparagus into the boiling water and cook for 4 to 8 minutes, depending on the size of the asparagus. ✪ Remove the asparagus and plunge into ice cold water. ✪ Allow the asparagus to cool and remove to a pan lined with paper towels. ✪ At serving time, heat the oil in a skillet large enough to hold the asparagus in a single layer. ✪ When the oil is hot, add the asparagus and sauté by shaking the pan and rolling the asparagus until heated through, about 3 minutes. ✪ Remove and set aside on a plate, and season with salt and pepper. ✪ Divide the asparagus among 4 plates and top with the Mescal Hollandaise.

Asparagus

Asparagus with Mescal Hollandaise

Mescal Hollandaise

YIELD: 1¹/₂ CUPS

Tequila is a variety of mescal that comes from a particular region around Jalisco, famed for its tequilas. Other regions in Mexico also make excellent mescals. My favorite mescal is Del Maguey. It's handmade by one of Oaxaca's top palenqueros, an old-fashioned mescal maker who ferments the heart of the maguey plant and distills his mescal in small batches. Use the best mescal. A good mescal will give a sauce like this one a wonderful herbal flavor.

3 large egg yolks
Juice of 1 lemon (about 2 tablespoons)
1 cup cold butter, cut into pieces
2 tablespoons mescal
Kosher salt to taste
Freshly ground pepper to taste

✪ This may be prepared in a saucepan directly over the heat, but it's easier not to ruin it if you use a stainless steel bowl placed over a saucepan of simmering water. ✪ In either method, combine the egg yolks and lemon juice and heat over low heat, whisking continuously until the mixture is light and creamy. ✪ Begin adding pieces of butter while whisking to blend. ✪ As the butter melts and emulsifies, add more. ✪ Keep adding and whisking until the butter is used up and the sauce is thick. ✪ Whisk in the mescal and season with salt and pepper. ✪ Serve at once.

The Hartnetts: A Cowboy Cooking Dynasty

★ ★ ★ ★ ★ ★ ★ ★ ★ ★ ★ ★ ★ ★ ★ ★ ★ ★ ★ ★

In the Trans-Pecos, the most famous name in cowboy cooking is Hartnett. Like the freckled vaquero named Obregon in *Giant*, who had a distant relative named O'Brien, the Hartnetts are a Mexican family with some Anglo blood mixed in somewhere, hence the English-sounding name.

Bobby McKnight, of the McKnight Ranch, and an old cowboy named Joe Richardson were sitting around the Reata bar one night arguing about which of the Hartnetts was the greatest cowboy cook. "Lalo Hartnett was good, but he was crazy," Bobby said. "I remember one time we were out doing a roundup for a whole month, and Lalo accidentally set his pants on fire the second day. They burned clear up to his knees before he could put the fire out. He cooked in those burned-up shorts for twenty-eight straight days. Never took them off. He was an ornery cuss, mean as hell, but boy he made great biscuits."

"Now Tommy Hartnett, over at the India Land and Cattle Company, he was a cook who knew how to bake biscuits. Touchy fellow though," said Joe. "I remember one time this green young cowboy asked him if he bought those biscuits at the Safeway. The kid was dead serious. He was going to tell his wife to pick some up next time she went shopping. Tommy ran him out of camp and never let him come back. I remember one time Tommy made picadillo for lunch. You know, ground meat and jalapeños and seasonings fried up in a Dutch oven and served with biscuits. I ate so damn much of that stuff I couldn't get back on my horse."

"I think Ramon Hartnett was the all-time best," said Bobby. "His food was clean, and he was just a nice guy to be around. His *pan de skillia* (skillet bread in Tex-Mex) and green chili were great and he never served the same stuff twice. Nothing pisses off cowboys like eating lunch for supper again. It's bad enough you have to eat beans for every meal.

"Frank Molinar, Ramon Hartnett's son, still cooks around here. He's the reigning king." You ought to taste his sourdough bread pudding with brandy sauce.

Corn Pudding Pie

Corn Pudding Pie

YIELD: 6 SERVINGS

Corn pudding baked in a pie shell is a simple but fancy-looking side dish. It also makes a nice light lunch alongside a Green Salad with Texas Goat Cheese and Spicy Pecans (page 136).

1/3 recipe Piecrust (page 175)
   or 1 9-inch prepared pie shell
1/2 cup minced red onion
1 tablespoon unsalted butter
1 cup cooked, drained, crumbled
   smoked bacon (about 1 pound uncooked)
2 cups corn kernels (cut from about 2 ears)
2/3 cup diced tomato (about 1 tomato)
1/2 cup grated Monterey Jack
4 eggs, lightly beaten
1/2 cup milk
1 tablespoon Pasilla Powder
   (page 196) or chile powder
3 tablespoons unsalted butter, melted
Kosher salt to taste
Freshly ground pepper to taste

✪ Roll out the piecrust dough to fit a 9-inch pie pan. ✪ Put the dough into the pan and trim and flute the edges. ✪ Set aside. ✪ Preheat the oven to 350°. ✪ Sauté the onions with 1 tablespoon of the butter for 4 minutes or until soft. ✪ Layer the bacon in the prepared piecrust; top it with the onion, corn, and tomato, then sprinkle with the cheese.

✪ In a small bowl, combine the eggs, milk, pasilla powder, and melted butter; blend with a whisk. ✪ Season with salt and pepper. ✪ Pour the egg mixture over the corn mixture. ✪ Place the pie pan on a flat baking sheet and put in the oven. ✪ Bake for 30 to 40 minutes or until pie is golden. ✪ The center should be set and a knife inserted near the center should be moist but clean when the pie is done. ✪ Remove from the oven and let sit about 5 minutes before serving.

Cheese and Bacon Grits

YIELD: 6 SERVINGS

Cheese and bacon grits make a nice Sunday brunch dish. Try them with a poached egg on top. They're also tasty, with meats and vegetables, for dinner.

4 cups chicken stock

3 tablespoons unsalted butter

$1^1/_2$ cups regular grits

1 cup cooked, drained, and crumbled
   smoked bacon (about 1 pound uncooked)

$1^3/_4$ cups grated caciotta or Monterey Jack

4 scallions, thinly sliced

1 tablespoon Tabasco™ Jalapeño Sauce

Kosher salt to taste

Freshly ground pepper to taste

✪ In a large, heavy saucepan, bring the chicken stock to a boil. ✪ Adjust the heat to a simmer. ✪ Add 1 tablespoon of the butter. ✪ When it has melted, begin to pour in the grits with one hand while constantly whisking with the other. ✪ When all of the grits have been stirred in, change to a long-handled wooden spoon and stir until the grits become thick and absorb the liquid. This should take from 7 to 10 minutes. ✪ Remove the saucepan from the heat and stir in the remaining 2 tablespoons butter, bacon, cheese, scallions, and Tabasco. ✪ Combine everything thoroughly and season with salt and pepper. ✪ Preheat the oven to 350°. ✪ Butter an 8-inch square pan, or other similar-sized baking pan, and spread the grits into the pan. ✪ Bake for 30 minutes, or until they are heated through. ✪ Serve hot.

Fried Grits

YIELD: VARIES

Leftover grits mold themselves into the shape of the container you refrigerate them in. If you put them in loaf pan, you'll get nice square slices. These are great for breakfast with scrambled eggs.

Leftover grits from Cheese and
   Bacon Grits (page 122)
$1/_4$ cup corn oil

✪ Chill leftover grits overnight. ✪ Remove them from the refrigerator and slice them into 1-inch-thick slices. ✪ Heat the oil in a heavy skillet. ✪ When the oil is very hot and almost smoking, slide the slices into the pan. ✪ Cook for 3 to 4 minutes, or until the slices brown and become crisp. ✪ Turn them once and continue cooking on the other side. ✪ Remove and drain on a paper towel. ✪ Serve hot.

Fried
Grits

Cabbage Braised in Texas Port

YIELD: 4 SERVINGS

Everybody thinks of Texas wine as something new, but in fact Texas has been producing wine since the 1800s. Val Verde, the oldest bonded winery in Texas, is famous for their port. Unfortunately, the supply is limited, so we use Messina Hof or Llano Estacado port to make this sweet and tender braised cabbage. Serve this with barbecued pork or any kind of sausage.

3 tablespoons vegetable oil

1 pound peppered bacon, coarsely chopped

1 red onion, chopped

4 cups julienned red cabbage

4 cups julienned green cabbage

3 green apples, cored and diced

3 cloves garlic, minced

2 tablespoons Pasilla Powder (page 196)

3 cups Texas port

✪ Heat the oil in a deep skillet with a lid. ✪ Add the bacon and onion. ✪ Cook for 6 minutes, or until the bacon starts to brown. ✪ Add the cabbage, apples, garlic, and pasilla. Cook for 4 minutes. ✪ Add the port, reduce heat to low, and cover. ✪ Simmer for 1 hour.

Braised Cabbage

Cabbage Braised in Texas Port

Refrigerator-Smoked Corn on the Cob

Refrigerator-Smoked Corn on the Cob with Chile Butter

YIELD: 4 SERVINGS

People don't like to eat corn on the cob in a restaurant, so we cut the smoked corn off the cob and toss it with Chile Butter. But at home, it's more fun to slather the whole ear with Chile Butter and eat it off the cob. This goes great with fried chicken.

4 ears fresh corn, shucked
4 tablespoons Chile Butter (see page 202)
Kosher salt to taste
Freshly ground pepper to taste

✪ Prepare an outdoor smoker as described on page 31, or use the directions for setting up a stove-top smoker that follow. ✪ If using a stove-top smoker, use $1^1/_2$ tablespoons of the "smoke dust" in the bottom. ✪ Fit the drip pan in the smoker (lined with foil) and pour $^1/_2$ cup water into the pan. ✪ Position the rack on top and place the ears of corn on it. ✪ Close the lid and place the smoker over high heat. ✪ When smoke begins to appear, reduce the heat to medium. ✪ Cook for 20 minutes, or until tender. ✪ If using an outdoor smoker, put a pan of water close to the smoke source so that the corn won't dry out. ✪ Serve with Chile Butter, salt, and pepper.

Smoked Corn

Coyote Chayote

YIELD: 4 SERVINGS

This pale green Mexican squash is a favorite south of the border. Usually you have to worry about overcooking squash, but this one is very firm— worry about undercooking it.

1 small jicama
2 chayote squash
2 large carrots
2 tablespoons unsalted butter
Kosher salt to taste
Freshly ground pepper to taste

✪ Cut off the rough outer skin of the jicama and peel the chayote and carrots. ✪ Julienne the vegetables. ✪ They should be 3 inches long and $1/8$ inch thick. ✪ Toss the vegetables to combine them. ✪ In a large, shallow sauté pan, heat the butter over high heat. ✪ When it is sizzling, add all of the vegetables and cook over high heat, stirring and tossing to keep the vegetables moving. ✪ The cooking time will be brief, approximately 5 to 6 minutes. ✪ Season with salt and pepper and serve at once.

7

Hallie Stillwell, ranch woman, writer, Justice of the Peace, 1897-1997

Ranch House Soups and Salads

MY WIFE AND I WERE MARRIED BY Justice of the Peace Hallie Stillwell. Hallie was a legend in the Trans-Pecos, one of the last of the old-time ranch women. Hallie and her daughter, Dadie, used to be regular customers at the Reata in Alpine. On Hallie's ninety-fifth birthday, I went out to her ranch in Stillwell to do a barbecue for her.

To get to the Stillwell Ranch, you drive about forty-five miles south of Marathon and turn off on a paved road that turns into a dirt road. Then the dirt road disappears, and you just keep driving through the dust and cactus another ten miles or so. It's one of the most desolate, primitive ranches I have ever seen.

When Hallie first arrived on the ranch in 1918, her husband, Roy, couldn't let her stay at home when he and his cowboys rode off to work because Pancho Villa and his band were terrorizing the area. So Hallie became one of the cowhands. She could track cattle on the open range, throw calves, and rope with the best of them. She shot a mountain lion one morning before breakfast.

In her book, *I'll Gather My Geese*, she remembers when she first tried to cook at the ranch. The cowboys ignored her. They always did their own cooking, and she soon found that she just got in their way. So one day she tried to do some housekeeping.

She scrubbed the dirty walls, which were covered with scribbles, and scoured out the filthy coffeepot, which had never been washed. When her husband and his two cowboys came home, she expected them to be impressed. Instead, they were furious. The scribblings were the only accounting records the ranch had ever kept, and every cowboy knew that cleaning a coffeepot ruined the coffee.

But, eventually, the cowboys came to appreciate Hallie's efforts to bring a little civilization to the place. She found a tree full of peaches at the family house in Marathon and hauled back a bushel to make peach preserves. She picked wildflowers and decorated the table with them. Hallie was always more of a cowhand than a housewife, but her story is a good illustration of how women changed cowboy life.

In the early days, women were rare in cattle country. Most ranch bosses wouldn't even hire married men to work as cowboys. But once the open range was fenced and cowboy life became less nomadic, ranchers and their hands began to marry.

It wasn't an easy life for women, and lots of old cowboys resented having them around. When Hallie moved to the Stillwell Ranch, the two cowboys that used to sleep in the one-room ranch house with her husband had to start bunking in the barn.

Some women worked cattle with the men, like Hallie did. But, sooner or later, most cowboy wives got pregnant and assumed more domestic duties. Hallie Stillwell never wanted to milk cows, or tend chickens, or cook; she wanted to ride with the cowboys. But raising small children kept her at home. It was a very lonely life. Working in the garden, churning butter, and making preserves were just ways to keep busy and stay sane during those home-bound years.

As more and more women came to live on ranches, cowboy chow came to include fresh eggs, garden vegetables, pickles, preserves, salads, and soups. With fresh butter on hand, the women could bake pies and cookies for dessert. The cowboys liked these "dainties," but still thought that some jobs, like making coffee and "tanning a steak," were better left to men.

Men and women sharing the cooking seems like a modern idea, but it was pretty common in Hallie Stillwell's day. The soups and salads in this chapter are popular first courses at the Reata. They aren't chuck-wagon dishes, but part of the ranch-house cooking tradition that was invented when western women and chuck-wagon cooks started working together in the kitchen.

Iceberg Quarters with Buttermilk Dressing

YIELD: 4 SERVINGS

Here's a salad you don't see much anymore. On a hot summer day in Texas, it's one of the most refreshing salads you can eat. And it's definitely the easiest. I like the iceberg ice cold!

1 head iceberg lettuce
2 cups Buttermilk Dressing (recipe follows)
Cracked pepper to taste (page 199)

✪ Cut the head of lettuce lengthwise into four quarters. ✪ Put each quarter on a salad plate. ✪ Pour $^1/_2$ cup of dressing over each quarter and sprinkle with pepper.

Buttermilk Dressing

YIELD: 2 CUPS

This is Reata's version of ranch dressing. The very idea of cowboys eating salads would send an old-fashioned pot-rassler into fits of hysterics. So it's kind of ironic that a salad dressing is the most famous example of ranch-style food. Of course, West Texans consider ranch dressing as more of an all-purpose sauce than a salad dressing anyway. I've seen folks pour it on everything from chicken-fried steak to breakfast biscuits.

$^1/_3$ cup minced red onion

2 scallions, thinly sliced

$^1/_2$ teaspoon Roasted Garlic (page 198)
   or minced garlic

$^1/_2$ teaspoon dried thyme leaves

1 cup sour cream

$^3/_4$ cup buttermilk

$^1/_2$ cup mayonnaise

Kosher salt to taste

Freshly ground pepper to taste

✪ Combine all of the ingredients in a bowl and blend with a whisk. The dressing is better if it is allowed to sit in the refrigerator for several hours to blend flavors before serving. ✪ Store it in the refrigerator in an airtight container; it will keep for about a week.

Green Salad with Texas Goat Cheese and Spicy Pecans

YIELD: 4 SERVINGS

With the largest goat population in the country, it's only natural that Texans would get involved in the goat cheese business. Larsen's and Yellow Rose are two outstanding Texas goat cheeses that go perfectly with a full-flavored salad like this one.

6 cups baby field greens (spring mix or mesclun)

1 cup Sherry Vinaigrette (recipe follows)

$1^1/_3$ cups soft goat cheese (about $^1/_2$ pound)

$1^1/_2$ cups Spicy Pecans (page 201)
or toasted pecans or walnuts

Kosher salt to taste

Freshly ground pepper to taste

✪ Place the greens in a large salad bowl and add the dressing. ✪ Toss to distribute the dressing evenly. ✪ Divide the mixture among 4 chilled salad plates. ✪ Drop teaspoonfuls of goat cheese around the edge of the salad, using $^1/_3$ cup for each serving. ✪ Sprinkle the salads with pecans, season with salt and pepper, and serve.

Green Salad

Green Salad with Texas Goat Cheese and Spicy Pecans

Sherry Vinaigrette

YIELD: 2 CUPS

This is our standard vinaigrette at Reata. If you use roasted shallots, you'll get a mellower flavor.

3 tablespoons Roasted Shallots (page 198)
   or 1 large shallot, minced
$^1/_3$ cup sherry wine vinegar
1 fresh egg
1 cup olive oil
$^1/_4$ teaspoon kosher salt
$^1/_2$ teaspoon freshly ground black pepper
1 tablespoon freshly squeezed lemon juice
Water as needed

✪ Place shallots and vinegar in a blender and purée. ✪ Add the egg and blend again. ✪ Remove the top and, with the motor running, drizzle the oil in very slowly. The dressing will emulsify and become thick. If it is too thick, thin it with water. ✪ Season the dressing with salt, pepper, and lemon juice.

Smoked Tomato Guacamole

YIELD: 4 SERVINGS

The smoked tomato adds a new dimension to this old favorite. Eat it as a dip with tortilla chips or on a bed of greens as a salad.

4 ripe avocados
1 cup minced red onion
1 cup diced Smoked Tomato (page 199)
  or 1 cup diced tomato
4 teaspoons freshly squeezed lemon juice
1 bunch cilantro, stemmed and chopped
Kosher salt to taste

✪ Cut an avocado in half. ✪ With a sharp knife, hit the pit so the blade sticks in the seed. ✪ Twist the knife slightly and remove and discard the pit. Cut the avocado into small dice. ✪ Scoop out the flesh into a bowl. ✪ Repeat with the remaining avocados.

✪ Add the onions and tomatoes to the avocados. ✪ Season with salt and lemon juice and add the cilantro. ✪ Mix the guacamole until everything is just incorporated. Serve at once, or hold with plastic wrap on the surface in a tightly covered container for a short time.

Smoked Tomato
Guacamole

Jicama and Carrot Coleslaw

Jicama and Carrot Coleslaw

YIELD: 6 SERVINGS

Martha Stewart Living *featured this crunchy slaw with grilled steaks,*
tamales, Ranch Beans (page 83), and Sourdough Onion Flatbread (page 90).

$^1/_2$ cup pineapple juice

2 tablespoons freshly squeezed lime juice

2 tablespoons olive oil

$^1/_4$ teaspoon ground coriander

Kosher salt to taste

Freshly ground pepper to taste

1 small jicama (about 1 pound)

4 carrots (about $^3/_4$ pound)

✪ In a bowl large enough to hold the completed salad, whisk together
the pineapple juice, lime juice, olive oil, coriander, salt, and pepper.
✪ Set aside.

✪ Cut off the rough outer skin of the jicama and peel the carrots.
✪ Julienne the vegetables. They should be about 3 inches long and
$^1/_8$ inch thick. ✪ Whisk the dressing again and toss gently with the prepared jicama and carrots. ✪ Adjust the seasoning with salt and pepper
as needed. ✪ Chill for a short time or serve immediately.

Cowtown Coleslaw

YIELD: 6 SERVINGS

This peppery slaw is colorful and it has as a zing to it. It's great with smoked meats and picnic fare.

5 cups julienned green cabbage
(about 1 head)
$1^1/_2$ cups julienned red cabbage
(about $^1/_3$ head)
2 carrots, peeled and julienned
5 jalapeño peppers, stemmed,
seeded, and julienned
$1^1/_4$ cups mayonnaise
$^1/_2$ cup malt vinegar
$^1/_2$ cup sugar
$1^1/_2$ tablespoons freshly squeezed lime juice
Kosher salt to taste
Freshly ground pepper to taste

✪ Place all of the vegetables in a large bowl. ✪ In another bowl, whisk together the mayonnaise, vinegar, sugar, and lime juice. ✪ Pour the dressing over the vegetables, season with salt and pepper, and toss to combine. ✪ Set aside in the refrigerator until serving time. It is best made and served on the same day.

Warm Potato Salad with Bacon Vinaigrette

YIELD: 4 TO 6 SERVINGS

German immigrants settled Central Texas around the same time as Stephen F. Austin's American families. They added a lot of German dishes, like this warm potato salad, to Texas cooking traditions.

2 $^1/_2$ pounds baby red potatoes

15 thin slices smoked bacon

1 cup diced red onion

$^3/_4$ cup olive oil

$^1/_2$ cup packed brown sugar

2 tablespoons cider vinegar

Kosher salt to taste

Freshly ground pepper to taste

✪ Place the potatoes in a pan and cover them with $1^1/_2$ inches of water. ✪ Bring the water to a boil, reduce the heat, and simmer for 20 minutes, or until the potatoes are just tender. ✪ While the potatoes are cooking, fry the bacon in a skillet until crisp and brown. Remove as cooked and drain on paper towels. ✪ Reserve 2 tablespoons of the bacon grease in the pan and quickly sauté the onion. ✪ Remove the onion and set aside. ✪ Crumble the bacon. You should have 1 cup of bacon pieces.

✪ When the potatoes have cooked, drain them and cut into quarters. ✪ Toss the potatoes with $^1/_4$ cup of the olive oil. ✪ Heat a grill to high temperature and grill the potatoes, turning to mark each side, and to finish the cooking. ✪ While the potatoes are cooking, combine the brown sugar and vinegar in a large salad bowl. ✪ Whisk to blend and dissolve the sugar. ✪ Slowly add the remaining $^1/_2$ cup oil, while continuing to whisk. ✪ Season with salt and pepper. ✪ Add the onions and bacon to the dressing. ✪ When the potatoes are ready, toss them with the dressing. ✪ Let the salad sit at room temperature for 30 minutes to allow the dressing to be absorbed. ✪ Serve warm.

Stacked Tomato and Sweet Onion Salad with Mango Vinaigrette

YIELD: 4 SERVINGS

I use big, ripe, summer beefsteak tomatoes from Fort Davis and supersweet Texas 1015 onions in this salad. You can use any vine-ripened tomato and sweet onions like Vidalias, Mauis, or Walla Wallas. But the size of the tomato and size of the onion should be about the same to make nice stacks.

2 avocados
8 $\frac{1}{2}$- inch-thick slices beefsteak tomato
8 $\frac{1}{2}$- inch-thick slices 1015 onion
2 cups Mango Vinaigrette (recipe follows)
12 sprigs cilantro, stemmed
Kosher salt to taste
Freshly ground pepper to taste

✪ Cut both avocados in half. ✪ Cut each half into three wedges, peeling as you go. Spread $\frac{1}{3}$ cup of the Mango Vinaigrette on four salad plates. ✪ Set a slice of tomato on the dressing, top with an onion slice, then tomato, and again an onion. ✪ Fan 3 avocado wedges on top of each stack. ✪ Drizzle with 2 tablespoons of the vinaigrette and garnish with 3 sprigs of cilantro. Season with salt and pepper.

Stacked Tomato and Sweet Onion Salad with Mango Vinaigrette

Mango Vinaigrette

YIELD: 4 CUPS

I use this spicy, tropical fruit salad dressing on all kinds of summer salads. Make some extra and keep a bottle in the fridge.

$^1/_2$ cup cider vinegar

2 teaspoons Dijon mustard

$^1/_2$ teaspoon minced garlic

$1^1/_2$ teaspoons honey

1 teaspoon freshly squeezed lime juice

1 cup peeled, ripe mango pieces plus

   $^1/_4$ cup peeled, finely diced ripe mango

$1^1/_2$ cups olive oil

$^1/_2$ cup minced cilantro leaves

$^1/_2$ habanero pepper, stemmed,

  seeded, and minced

2 tablespoons thinly sliced scallions

Kosher salt to taste

✪ Put the vinegar, mustard, garlic, honey, lime juice, and 1 cup ripe mango in a blender. ✪ Blend at medium speed. ✪ With the motor running, remove the top and slowly drizzle in the olive oil. The mixture should be thick and emulsified. ✪ Fold the cilantro, habaneros, scallions, and diced mango into the dressing. If the dressing is too thick, thin with water. ✪ Serve at once or store the dressing; it will keep for up to 4 days.

Cream of Carrot Soup

YIELD: 4 SERVINGS

Shirley Rooney taught me how to make this old-fashioned ranch-house soup. The pasilla chile powder gives it a deep color and a rich flavor.

4 carrots, coarsely chopped
$1/_2$ onion, coarsely chopped
4 garlic cloves
$1^1/_2$ cups chicken stock
$2^1/_2$ cups heavy cream
1 teaspoon Pasilla Powder (page 196)
Kosher salt to taste
Cracked Pepper to taste (page 199)

✪ Place the carrots, onion, garlic, and chicken stock in a saucepan. ✪ Bring to a boil and cook for 10 to 15 minutes, or until carrots are tender. ✪ Remove from heat and purée in a blender. ✪ Place mixture back in a saucepan and add the cream and Pasilla Powder. ✪ Simmer to reduce by one fourth. ✪ Season with salt. ✪ Garnish each serving with cracked pepper.

Cream of Jalapeño Soup

Cream of Jalapeño Soup

YIELD: 6 SERVINGS

This pepper bisque is Reata's most popular soup by a long shot. We get six or seven requests for this recipe every day.

5 jalapeño peppers, stemmed and seeded
1$^1/_2$ tablespoons unsalted butter
$^3/_4$ cup finely chopped red onion
   (about $^1/_2$ large onion)
3 cloves garlic, minced
1 avocado, peeled and diced
2 cups diced tomatoes
   (about 2 large tomatoes)
8 cups heavy cream
1 bunch cilantro, stemmed and chopped
Kosher salt to taste
Freshly ground pepper to taste

✪ Mince the jalapeños and set aside. In a large, heavy saucepan, heat the butter over medium heat. ✪ Add the jalapeños, onions, and garlic and sauté, stirring, until the vegetables are soft. ✪ Remove the pan from the heat and stir in the avocado, tomatoes, and cream. ✪ Lower the temperature and return the pan to the heat, watching and stirring so the cream does not separate. ✪ Bring the soup slowly back to a simmer and cook for about 30 minutes to reduce by one third and to blend the flavors. Be sure to stir the soup occasionally to prevent sticking or scorching. ✪ Season with salt and pepper. Just before serving stir the chopped cilantro leaves into the soup, reserving some for garnish. ✪ Ladle soup into bowls and garnish with remaining cilantro.

Tortilla Soup

YIELD: 4 SERVINGS

The secret to tortilla soup is to add the crispy tortilla strip "noodles" at the last minute so they don't get soggy. The best way to do this is to put out all the ingredients on a sideboard or at the table and let each person assemble their own soup.

1 whole chicken (about 3 pounds)

6 chicken wings

6 chicken legs or thighs

6 cloves garlic

4 shallots

1 tablespoon whole black peppercorns

1 carrot

3 to 4 quarts water

Kosher salt to taste

Freshly ground pepper to taste

2 avocados, peeled, seeded, and
   sliced lengthwise into eighths

2 jalapeño peppers, stemmed, seeded,
   and minced

$^1/_4$ cup oil

6 fresh corn tortillas, cut into thin strips

2 cups (about 8 ounces) grated
   Monterey Jack

1 lime, cut into sixths

$^1/_2$ bunch cilantro, stemmed,
   for garnish

✪ In a large, heavy, deep pan place the washed chicken and chicken pieces. Add the garlic, shallots, peppercorns, carrot, and water. The water should barely cover the chicken. ✪ Adjust the amount of water, if necessary. ✪ Place the pan over medium-high heat and bring to a boil. As the water begins to heat, skim any foam that rises to the surface and discard.

Tortilla Soup cont.

✪ When the water begins to boil, turn the heat down to a constant simmer. ✪ Continue skimming as necessary. ✪ Place the cover of the pan slightly ajar and continue cooking for $1^{1}/_{2}$ hours. ✪ Turn the heat off and let the chicken sit in the broth for $^{1}/_{2}$ hour to cool. ✪ When the chicken is cool enough to handle, pull the meat off of the bones, discarding the skin and bones. There should be about 3 cups of meat. ✪ Set the meat aside in a covered container that can be heated at serving time. ✪ Strain the broth and return it to a clean saucepan. ✪ Skim off any fat that has accumulated on the surface. There should be about 2 quarts of broth. ✪ Season with salt and pepper.

✪ At serving time, reheat the chicken. ✪ Heat the broth to boiling and keep hot. ✪ Prepare all of the vegetables. If you have sensitive skin, wear gloves when handling the hot peppers. In a large skillet, heat the oil. ✪ When the oil is hot, add the tortilla strips and sauté until crisp, turning them once or twice. ✪ Remove the strips and drain them on paper towels. ✪ Repeat if necessary. ✪ Have all of the soup ingredients ready to assemble at serving time, as you will "build" each soup bowl individually. ✪ In the bottom of the bowl, place $^{3}/_{4}$ cup chicken meat. ✪ Arrange avocado slices around the meat. ✪ Sprinkle with $^{1}/_{2}$ cup cheese, diced jalapeño, and top with a wedge of lime. ✪ Ladle hot broth over all and place a handful of crispy tortilla strips in the center. ✪ Top with a garnish of cilantro leaves. ✪ Serve at once.

Spicy Tomato Soup with Sourdough Croutons

YIELD: 4 SERVINGS

Adding a little baking soda to the tomatoes tones down the acids and gives this soup an old-fashioned flavor.

5 plum tomatoes, cut in half
  (about $1^1/_4$ pounds)
15 cloves garlic, minced
1 small red onion, thinly sliced
1 tablespoon dried thyme
$^1/_4$ teaspoon dried basil
1 teaspoon kosher salt
$1^1/_2$ teaspoons freshly ground pepper
2 tablespoons balsamic vinegar
1 tablespoon olive oil
2 teaspoons packed brown sugar
$^1/_2$ cup tomato juice
$^1/_2$ cup tomato purée
$^1/_2$ teaspoon baking soda
$1^1/_2$ cups heavy cream
Sourdough Croutons (recipe follows)

✪ Preheat oven to 350°. ✪ Place the cut tomatoes in a shallow baking dish with sides, just large enough to hold them. ✪ Cover the tomatoes with the garlic, onion, thyme, basil, salt, pepper, vinegar, oil, and sugar. ✪ Cover the pan with foil and roast in the oven for 30 minutes, or until the vegetables are tender. ✪ Remove the pan from the oven and let it cool slightly. ✪ Place the mixture in a blender. ✪ Purée, then strain into a large saucepan. You should have about $2^1/_4$ cups of tomato broth. ✪ Add the tomato juice, tomato purée, and baking soda and stir well. Add the cream. ✪ Bring the soup to a boil over medium heat, reduce heat, and simmer for 20 minutes to blend the flavors and reduce the soup. ✪ Serve hot, garnished with Sourdough Croutons.

Spicy Tomato Soup with Sourdough Croutons

Sourdough Croutons

YIELD: 2 CUPS

This is a great way to use up stale sourdough bread.

2 Sourdough Onion Flatbreads (page 90),
   or enough sourdough bread for 2 cups
   of 1-inch cubes

$^1/_4$ cup olive oil

1 teaspoon dried oregano leaves

1 teaspoon dried thyme leaves

1 teaspoon freshly ground pepper

✪ Preheat oven to 350°. ✪ Place the cut-up bread in a large bowl. In a small bowl, combine the oil with the oregano, thyme, and pepper. ✪ Drizzle this mixture over the bread and toss to evenly distribute the oil. ✪ Spread the seasoned cubes on a sheet pan large enough to hold the bread in a single layer. ✪ Bake for 30 minutes, or until the croutons are light brown and very crisp. ✪ Toss and mix the bread from time to time for even browning. ✪ Remove the croutons from the oven and let them cool. ✪ Use at once or store in an airtight container until needed.

8

The Lazy Susan: Peppers, Pickles, and Relishes

I THINK THE TRADITION OF HAVING lots of little bowls of condiments on the table is something we picked up from the Mexicans. In most ranch houses, they put all the pickles, relishes, and pepper sauces in the middle of the table on a lazy susan. Everybody loves to spoon and shake and sprinkle them all over everything. Sometimes, I sit down to the table and just roll up the peppers and relishes in flour tortillas and eat them plain.

Hot sauces and chile peppers were the original cowboy condiments. Cowboys never ran short of peppers because the tiny *pequín* chile grows wild all over South Texas. The birds eat the tiny peppers and "plant" new ones all over the place. You can pick the peppers green in the fall, or wait until they turn red around December. Then you put the peppers in a bottle of vinegar to keep them for the rest of the year, or you can dry them.

J. Frank Dobie used to carry a couple of dried *pequíns* in a snuff box so he'd always have some to season his food with. I've seen customers at the Reata pull out little silver pill boxes with dried *pequíns* in them too.

Down in the Lower Rio Grande and over in Mexico where it doesn't freeze very often, the *pequín* plants grow into enormous bushes. I found a big *pequín* bush last year while I was duck hunting on the Mexican coast south of Brownsville. I had been sitting in a duck blind since dawn, and I hadn't seen a single duck. Then I noticed that the blind was about ten feet away from this huge *pequín* chile bush. It was taller than I am, the biggest *pequín* bush I'd ever seen. I figured I'd rather pick those chiles than sit there with a shotgun in my lap all day, so I got out my canvas game sack and starting filling it up. I must have picked two pounds of chile *pequíns*.

I took them back to the hunting camp, and the Mexican ladies who cooked there oohed and aahed over them. I think they were more impressed by the chiles than they would have been if I'd brought back a duck. The chiles were unbelievably hot. I took them home and put them in a jar with some vinegar.

> The original purpose of all these pickled vegetables, relishes, and jams was to turn cheap and plentiful garden produce into something you could enjoy all year long.

The vinegar from the chiles makes a great pepper sauce, and you can keep refilling the jar with more vinegar when it gets low. You can also spoon out some *pequíns* when you want to add peppers to your cooking. J. Frank Dobie used to say that the best way to eat beans was to mash three or four chile *pequíns* in a bowl, add some plain-cooked pinto beans, and then put a little chopped onion on top.

Homemade pickled *pequíns* are one of those condiments that you often see on ranch-house tables along with pickles, pickled onions, salsa, relishes, and, of course, ketchup. The original purpose of all these pickled vegetables, relishes, and jams was to turn cheap and plentiful garden produce into something you could enjoy all year long. With the recipes in this chapter, you ought to be able to stock a fine-looking lazy susan.

Jose's Jalapeños

YIELD: 3 QUARTS

Pickled jalapeños are always found on Mexican and Texan tables. We named this version after Jose Falcon's little restaurant in Boquillas. Jalapeños are easy to grow in home gardens. One or two good plants will usually supply enough pickled peppers to last you a whole year.

30 jalapeño peppers (about $^3/_4$ pound)
25 cloves garlic
2 carrots (about $^1/_3$ pound),
   peeled and cut on the diagonal
1 red onion, peeled and cut into wedges
3 cups cider vinegar
2 cups pineapple juice
2 tablespoons whole peppercorns
2 teaspoons dried oregano leaves
3 sprigs thyme
2 bay leaves
1 teaspoon kosher salt

✪ Place the jalapeños, garlic, carrots, and onion in a large bowl. ✪ Pour the vinegar and pineapple juice into a saucepan and add the peppercorns, oregano, thyme, bay leaves, and salt. ✪ Heat the mixture to boiling. Pour the hot liquid over the jalapeños, stir to combine the ingredients, and place a plate or the pan itself on top of the peppers to keep them submerged in the hot liquid. ✪ Let cool to room temperature. ✪ Transfer the mixture to a 2-quart jar with a lid. ✪ Set aside in the refrigerator for 24 hours before serving.

Bread and Butter Pickles

YIELD: 2 QUARTS

This is one of the most popular styles of pickles in ranch houses around West Texas. We serve them with all our sandwiches at Reata.

2 pounds small pickling cucumbers
   (enough for 5 cups sliced)

1 1015 onion

5 cloves garlic, thinly sliced

4 cups cider vinegar

2 cups packed brown sugar

$1^1/_2$ tablespoons whole black peppercorns

1 tablespoon dried dillweed

$1^1/_2$ tablespoons dried yellow mustard seed

1 tablespoon whole allspice

1 teaspoon cardamom

$^1/_2$ teaspoon whole cloves

4 serrano chiles or other small,
   hot, red peppers

2 whole bay leaves

$^1/_2$ teaspoon ground turmeric

1 tablespoon kosher salt

✪ Wash the cucumbers well and slice them $^1/_8$ inch thick on the diagonal. Place the slices in a glass or stainless steel container. ✪ Peel and slice the onion into $^1/_8$-inch rings and add them to the cucumbers. ✪ Add the thinly sliced garlic. ✪ Pour the vinegar into a saucepan and add all of the remaining ingredients. ✪ Heat the mixture to boiling. ✪ Pour the hot liquid over the cucumbers and let cool to room temperature. ✪ Transfer the pickles to a jar with a lid and set them in the refrigerator for 24 hours before serving.

Pickled Texas 1015s

YIELD: 2 QUARTS

Lots of 1015 onions are grown in Presidio, near Alpine. These supersweet onions are only on the market for a month or so in the spring, so it's a good idea to pickle some to keep on hand for the rest of the year. You can use Vidalias, Walla Wallas, Mauis, or any other sweet onion if you're not lucky enough to have real Texas 1015s.

3 1015 onions, peeled and sliced
    into $\frac{1}{8}$-inch rings
8 cloves garlic
$2\frac{1}{2}$ cups cider vinegar
$\frac{1}{2}$ cup red wine
$\frac{1}{2}$ cup packed brown sugar
3 sprigs thyme
2 bay leaves
1 tablespoon whole peppercorns
$1\frac{1}{2}$ teaspoons yellow mustard seed
$1\frac{1}{2}$ teaspoons whole allspice
$\frac{1}{2}$ teaspoon ground cardamom
$\frac{1}{4}$ teaspoon ground cloves

✪ Place the onions and garlic in a large bowl. ✪ Pour the vinegar into a saucepan and add all of the remaining ingredients. ✪ Heat the liquid to boiling and pour it over the onions. ✪ Stir to blend all of the ingredients. Let the mixture cool to room temperature. ✪ Stir again and transfer the mixture to a 2-quart jar with a lid. ✪ Set in the refrigerator for 24 hours before serving.

Pickled Texas 1015s

Shaker-Bottle Pepper Sauce

Robb has a wild pequin *bush in his backyard, but for most folks,* chile pequin *are hard to find. Mexicans harvest them wild down in Sonora and sell them in Mexican markets every fall, but* pequins *don't cross the border much. If you don't have your own* chile pequin *bush, you can substitute cayenne, tabasco, serrano, or just about any other fresh hot pepper in this recipe. In the Caribbean, they make a sauce just like this with habaneros.*

$^1/_2$ cup pequin chiles or other fresh peppers
$^1/_2$ cup white vinegar

✪ Clean a previously used pepper shaker bottle with boiling water. (For larger peppers, such as serranos or habaneros, double the ingredients and use a pancake syrup dispenser.) ✪ Pack the bottle with chiles. ✪ Heat the vinegar in a small saucepan over low heat until it steams slightly. ✪ Pour the vinegar over the chiles to the top of the jar. ✪ Allow the mixture to sit for a day before using.

✪ You can use the vinegar as a pepper sauce, or open the bottle to take out a few chiles. ✪ The bottle can be refilled with vinegar about 3 times. It keeps refrigerated for 6 months or more.

Shaker-Bottle Pepper Sauces

Pickled Pico de Gallo

YIELD: ABOUT 2 CUPS

If you use Jose's Jalapeños (page 159) for this recipe, you'll get a nice sweet flavor that adds a new twist to this popular salsa.

5 pickled jalapeño peppers, stemmed,
   seeded, and minced
1 cup diced tomatoes
1 cup chopped red onion
$^1/_2$ cup coarsely chopped cilantro leaves
1 tablespoon freshly squeezed lemon juice
Kosher salt to taste

✪ In a bowl, combine the jalapeños, tomatoes, onions, and cilantro. ✪ Add the lemon juice and salt and mix. ✪ Serve at once or cover and hold in the refrigerator for a couple of days.

Salsa Verde

YIELD: 2 CUPS

This green sauce is one of the most popular table salsas in Mexico and Texas. It also makes a great sauce for green enchiladas.

1 pound tomatillos (about 13)
$^1/_4$ bunch cilantro, stems removed,
   leaves chopped
3 fresh serrano chiles, stemmed and chopped
$^1/_2$ cup thinly sliced scallions
   (about 5 scallions)
$1^1/_2$ teaspoons minced garlic
$^1/_4$ cup red bell pepper, cut into $^1/_8$-inch dice
2 tablespoons honey
1 teaspoon freshly squeezed lime juice
Kosher salt to taste

✪ Husk the tomatillos by removing the parchmentlike covering on the outside. ✪ Rinse them and place them in a saucepan. ✪ Just cover them with water. ✪ Bring the water to a boil, reduce the heat, and allow the tomatillos to simmer for 3 to 5 minutes, or until they are just tender but still green in color. ✪ Remove them from heat, drain them, and coarsely chop them in a food processor. ✪ Pour the tomatillos into a bowl and add the cilantro, chiles, scallions, garlic, bell pepper, honey, and lime juice. Mix well. ✪ Season with salt. Will keep for up to a week in the refrigerator.

Salsa Verde

Reata Ranchero Sauce

YIELD: APPROXIMATELY 3 CUPS

This basic ranchero sauce is perfect for huevos rancheros or meatloaf and mashed potatoes.

4 cloves garlic, chopped

3 jalapeño peppers, stemmed, seeded,
  and chopped

5 Smoked Tomatoes, chopped (page 199)

1 red onion, chopped

$1/_4$ cup cilantro leaves

$1/_2$ cup olive oil

2 cups chicken stock

Kosher salt to taste

Freshly ground pepper to taste

✪ Combine the garlic, peppers, tomatoes, onion, and cilantro in a food processor. ✪ Pulse the motor to coarsely grind the mixture. ✪ In a large, shallow skillet, heat the oil over medium-high heat. ✪ Pour the chopped vegetable mixture into the pan and cook for 5 minutes. ✪ Blend in the chicken stock, bring it to a boil, and reduce the heat. ✪ Simmer the mixture for about 30 minutes to reduce and thicken. ✪ Season with salt and pepper. Serve at once or store in the refrigerator. ✪ Keeps up to 4 days.

Apple-Poblano Chutney

YIELD: 3 1/2 CUPS

We serve this Wild West chutney on Oven-Roasted Tenderloin of Pork (page 29) at the Reata, but it's also great on grilled lamb chops, venison, steaks, or even a bagel with cream cheese.

1 tablespoon unsalted butter

1 cup peeled, cored, diced Granny Smith
  apples (about 1 large apple)

1 cup diced red onion (about 1/2 onion)

3 cloves garlic, minced

1/2 cup Roasted Poblano Peppers, diced
  (see page 195)

1/2 cup white wine

1 cup Jalapeño Jelly (page 170)

1/2 cup julienned fresh sage leaves

Kosher salt to taste

Freshly ground pepper to taste

✪ Heat 1 tablespoon of butter in a large, nonstick sauté pan over medium heat. ✪ Add the apples, onions, and garlic, and cook for about 5 minutes, or until they are just beginning to soften. ✪ Blend in the poblanos and sauté briefly. ✪ Pour in the wine and cook until the wine has reduced, shaking or stirring to prevent sticking. ✪ Add the jelly and stir until jelly has melted. ✪ The mixture will be thick and jam-like. ✪ Remove the pan from the heat, fold in the sage, and season with salt and pepper. ✪ Set aside until serving time. Chutney may be served warm or at room temperature.

Onion Marmalade

YIELD: 5 CUPS

This is one of my all-time favorite relishes. It's also a great garnish or topping for just about any kind of meat dish.

2 large red onions (about $1^1/_2$ pounds)
2 large yellow onions (about $1^1/_2$ pounds)
4 bunches scallions, green part only
3 tablespoons olive oil
$1^1/_2$ cups balsamic vinegar
$^1/_4$ cup brown sugar
Kosher salt to taste
Freshly ground pepper to taste

✪ Peel the onions and trim the root ends. ✪ Stand each onion on its root end and slice through the center top to bottom. ✪ Continue thinly slicing each half in this fashion to produce thin, semicircular julienne slices. ✪ Slice the green part of the scallions into thin slices. ✪ Heat the olive oil in a large skillet over medium heat. ✪ Add all of the onions and scallions and toss to coat with oil. ✪ Sauté until onions begin to soften. ✪ Cover the pan and cook until they are wilted. ✪ Remove the lid, increase the heat, and add the vinegar. ✪ Cook until the vinegar reduces by one half, stirring occasionally. ✪ Add the sugar, salt, and pepper and stir well. Taste the mixture; it should be sweet and sour. Onions have different amounts of natural sugar at different times of the year, so the amount of sugar may need to be adjusted to taste. ✪ Reduce to low heat and continue cooking the mixture until the liquid is almost absorbed and the marmalade is thick, about 10 minutes. ✪ Remove from heat and serve. ✪ Store any extra in a jar in the refrigerator; it will keep up to a week.

Onion Marmalade

Sun-Dried Tomato–Goat Cheese Pesto

YIELD: ABOUT 2 CUPS

At Reata we use this on portobello mushroom sandwiches and our chicken burritos, but it works fine on pasta like any other pesto.

15 sun-dried tomato halves
5 teaspoons Roasted Garlic (see page 198)
1 jalapeño pepper, stemmed and seeded
$^1/_2$ cup (packed) fresh spinach leaves, stemmed
$^1/_2$ cup soft goat cheese
$^2/_3$ cup olive oil
Kosher salt to taste
Freshly ground pepper to taste

✪ Place the sun-dried tomatoes in a bowl and pour boiling water over them. ✪ Let them sit for 10 to 15 minutes to rehydrate. ✪ Drain them well. ✪ Put the garlic, jalapeño, spinach, drained tomatoes, and goat cheese in a food processor and purée. ✪ With the motor running, pour the oil through the feed tube in a steady stream until well blended. ✪ Remove the pesto from the bowl and serve it at once, or store it in the refrigerator. ✪ Bring the pesto back to room temperature before serving.

Jalapeño Jelly

YIELD: 6 8-OUNCE JARS

We use this as a glaze for grilled meats, but it's really good on hot biscuits too.

12 jalapeño peppers, stemmed and seeded
1$^1/_2$ cups cider vinegar
6 cups sugar
6 ounces liquid fruit pectin

✪ If you have sensitive skin, wear gloves when handling the hot peppers. ✪ Place the jalapeños in a blender. ✪ Pour the vinegar over them and blend to purée the peppers. ✪ Transfer the pepper liquid to a large saucepan and add the sugar. ✪ Stir together and bring to a boil over medium heat. ✪ Continue to cook and stir for 5 minutes, or until the sugar dissolves. ✪ Remove the liquid from the heat and let it cool for 10 minutes. ✪ At that time, blend the pectin into the jalapeño mixture. ✪ Remove any foam from the top of the jelly with a spoon. ✪ Pour the jelly into 8-ounce jars. Put lids on the jars and store until needed.

Ancho Ketchup

YIELD: ABOUT 5 CUPS

Try this on your french fries, onion rings, and hamburgers and you'll never go back to the tomato kind.

12 ancho chili peppers, stemmed and seeded
$1/_2$ white onion, diced
5 cloves garlic, minced
6 cups water
5 teaspoons packed brown sugar
2 tablespoons ground cumin
2 cups tomato paste
Kosher salt to taste
Freshly ground pepper to taste

✪ Place the peppers, onion, and garlic in a large saucepan and cover with the water. Bring to a boil over high heat, reduce heat, and simmer for about 15 minutes, or until the peppers have absorbed some liquid and have become soft. ✪ Remove the peppers, onion, and garlic with a slotted spoon and transfer them to a food processor. ✪ Add the brown sugar, cumin, tomato paste, and 1 cup of the liquid the peppers were cooked in. ✪ Puréc, adding more pepper liquid until you reach the desired thickness. ✪ Adjust seasonings with salt, pepper, and more brown sugar if desired. ✪ Spoon the ketchup into a glass container and store it in the refrigerator until ready for use.

9

Pies, Sweets, and Cowboy Coffee

COWBOYS HAVE ALWAYS BEEN WEAK FOR SWEETS. Anything that vaguely resembles dessert usually gets a wild reception in cowboy country—but pie is the one thing cowboys really go crazy over. An old cowboy cook once said that you could fix up anything, call it pie, sink it in the Rio Grande, and every cowboy in the county would drown diving after it.

It's hard to bake a pie over a campfire, so pie was pretty rare in the chuck-wagon days. The kind of desserts that came from Dutch ovens were usually canned fruit and sourdough cobblers or spotted pup. Spotted pup is rice or bread pudding seasoned with cinnamon and "spotted" with raisins.

Pies didn't become common until the ranch-house era. Women probably baked most pies, but some old cowboys were pretty proud of their pies back then too, and some still are today. There's a retired Texas Ranger named Joaquin Jackson who comes into the Reata in Alpine a lot. He's a tall, rugged-looking, no-nonsense hombre who chased crooks and cattle rustlers all his life, but he'd also be the first to tell you that he bakes a mean buttermilk pie.

But when I think of crackerjack pie bakers, I think of ranch women like Shirley Rooney, who worked with me at the Gage Hotel. Shirley baked all our breads and all

Texas Ranger Joaquin Jackson

our desserts. We set her up a little bakery down in the basement; she called it "the hole." It turned out to be a pretty smart setup because, when Shirley was upstairs, nobody got any work done. Shirley could talk for an hour about the weather on a day when there wasn't a cloud in the sky. She knew everybody in the Trans-Pecos and all the latest gossip. We had to send her down to "the hole" sometimes just to rest our ears.

Shirley was quite a character, and her buttermilk pies were awesome. I could never get enough of them. Every time she baked them, the guys in the kitchen would take turns stealing one. Shirley always baked ten pies in a batch, and she always left them to out to cool for a while on a baker's rack. One guy would sneak into the basement, snitch a hot pie, and rush it to the kitchen where we would stick it in the freezer. Then we'd cover it up with freezer paper and write "sirloin" or something on it. We'd wait until it was nice and cold—that's when buttermilk pie tastes best—and then we'd each grab a fork and devour the whole thing.

Our pie rustling drove Shirley crazy. She'd come looking for her missing pie in the kitchen and stand there yelling at us while we all stood there grinning. I'm sure she knew what we were doing, but I think Shirley liked to yell as much as she liked to talk. I learned more about pies and sweets from Shirley Rooney than from anybody else, and these recipes include a lot of her inspirations. But I'll warn you now that if the desserts in this chapter turn out as good as hers, you better hide them while they're cooling.

Piecrust

YIELD: 3 9-INCH CIRCLES OR 2 RECTANGULAR CRUSTS

The cake flour in this piecrust recipe makes it a little different from most. I think it gives the crust a great texture. You can use butter-flavored Crisco as the solid vegetable shortening. It also comes in sticks, which makes measuring easier.

1 cup unsalted butter

1 cup solid vegetable shortening

4 cups cake flour

2 cups all-purpose flour

$^1/_2$ cup sugar

3 teaspoons kosher salt

$^1/_4$ to $^1/_2$ cup cold water

✪ In a mixer fitted with paddle attachment, combine the butter, shortening, 2 cups of the cake flour, and 1 cup of the all-purpose flour. ✪ Blend together on low speed for 2 minutes. ✪ Stop the mixer and scrape the sides of the bowl. ✪ Add the remaining 2 cups cake flour and the remaining 1 cup all-purpose flour. ✪ Blend to combine completely. ✪ Mix the sugar and salt into $^1/_4$ cup of the water and add it to the flour mixture. ✪ Blend briefly and add the remaining water if needed. The dough should not be overworked and should make a solid piece when held in your hand. ✪ Turn the dough out onto a lightly floured smooth surface and knead it several times. ✪ Divide the dough into portions and flatten it. ✪ Wrap the dough in plastic and either chill it before rolling out or freeze for future use.

✪ When needed, thaw. Gather pastry into a ball. Press into the bottom and sides of a 9-inch pie pan or a 9 by 13-inch rectangular pan, ensuring the sides are covered. ✪ If shell or piecrust needs prebaking, heat oven to 475°. ✪ Prick bottom and sides of pastry thoroughly with fork. Bake them to 12 minutes or until light brown. Cool on wire rack.

Piecrust

Buttermilk Pie with Rum-Soaked Raisins

YIELD: 6 TO 8 SERVINGS

Also known as Buttermilk Chess Pie, this is the granddaddy of West Texas pies, probably because buttermilk was the one pie filling you could always get. The rum raisin filling is my own little twist.

$1/_2$ cup dark raisins

$1/_2$ cup golden raisins

$1/_2$ cup spiced rum

$1/_3$ recipe Piecrust (page 175)

$1^3/_4$ cups sugar

1 tablespoon flour

4 eggs

8 tablespoons unsalted butter, softened

1 cup buttermilk

1 tablespoon freshly squeezed lime juice

2 teaspoons pure vanilla extract

1 tablespoon ground nutmeg

✪ Combine the raisins and rum in a container and set them aside for 12 hours to soften, stirring occasionally.

✪ Roll out the piecrust dough to fit a 9-inch pie pan. ✪ Put the dough into the pan, trim and flute the edges. ✪ Set aside. ✪ Preheat the oven to 350°. ✪ In a metal bowl, combine the sugar and flour. ✪ In another bowl, lightly beat the eggs and add them to the sugar mixture, combining well. ✪ Blend the butter into the mixture using the back of a spoon. ✪ Add the buttermilk and blend with a whisk. If the butter has not incorporated by this step, set the bowl over a pan of simmering water to help soften the butter. ✪ Add the lime juice, vanilla, and nutmeg. ✪ Blend well. ✪ Drain and sprinkle the raisins in the bottom of the prepared piecrust and slowly pour the custard filling over them. ✪ Set the pie on a baking sheet and place it in the oven for 1 hour to 1 hour and 15 minutes. The pie will not be runny in the middle when cooking is complete. A knife inserted into the center will come out moist but clean when the pie is cooked. ✪ Remove the pie and let it cool before cutting.

Pecan Pie

YIELD: 8 SERVINGS

Pecans are native to Texas. We have a good many pecan trees in the river bottoms of the Trans-Pecos. During the fall, everybody collects sacks of them. I know one woman who encourages her sons and husband to watch football games every Saturday and Sunday in the fall—but she makes them shell pecans while they sit in front of the TV.

$^1/_2$ recipe Piecrust (page 175)

6 eggs

$^1/_2$ cup sugar

$^1/_2$ cup flour

4 cups dark corn syrup

$1^1/_2$ teaspoons pure vanilla extract

$^1/_2$ teaspoon kosher salt

2 cups chopped pecans

✪ Preheat the oven to 400°. ✪ Lightly butter an 8 by 12-inch pie pan. Roll out the piecrust dough to fit the pan. ✪ Put the dough into the pan, trim and flute the edges. ✪ Set aside.

✪ In a mixer with a paddle attachment, beat the eggs until well combined and light in color, about 5 minutes. ✪ Mix the sugar and flour together and gradually add to the eggs using low speed. ✪ Add the corn syrup, vanilla, and salt and blend well, again using low speed. ✪ Fold the nuts in by hand and pour the mixture into the prepared piecrust. ✪ Bake at 400° for 10 minutes and then reduce the heat to 350° and bake for 1 hour longer. The pie will rise up and form cracks on the top, and the filling will be set when baking is complete. ✪ Add additional time if the center looks too runny. A knife inserted into the center will come out moist but clean when the pie is cooked. ✪ Remove from the oven and let cool before serving.

Pecan Pie

Refrigerator Chocolate Pie with Caramelized Bananas

YIELD: 6 SERVINGS

This is a chocolate-lover's dream pie, and the dark, rich chocolate-cream filling is sensational with the candied bananas. Note that this recipe uses uncooked eggs. Small children, the very elderly, and others with compromised immune systems should take caution in eating anything containing raw eggs, although every step is taken to ensure healthful eggs in our restaurants and supermarkets. If you have any questions, contact your physician.

1 cup unsalted butter

$1^1/_2$ cups superfine granulated sugar

6 eggs

$1^1/_2$ tablespoons pure vanilla extract

2 teaspoons almond extract

1 cup sifted cocoa powder

1 prebaked 8-inch piecrust (page 175)

1 recipe Caramelized Bananas (recipe follows)

✪ Cream the butter and sugar in a mixer fitted with a balloon whisk (or use a hand-held mixer) until light in color and texture. ✪ Add the eggs one at a time, beating well after each addition. ✪ Blend in the extracts and sift the cocoa over the creamed mixture. ✪ Set the mixer speed on medium-low and beat for 30 minutes. The mixture will be light and an intense chocolate color. ✪ Pour or scrape the mixture into the piecrust and refrigerate the pie for 24 hours before serving. If you cover it with plastic wrap it will leave marks on the top of the pie; it is better to leave the pie uncovered or cover with something that will not touch the surface. ✪ Serve with the Caramelized Bananas.

Caramelized Bananas

YIELD: ABOUT 3 CUPS

We use these on chocolate pie, but they also make an outrageous banana split.

$^3/_4$ **cup packed brown sugar**
$^3/_4$ **cup cold unsalted butter, cut into pieces**
4 bananas, diced

✪ Heat the brown sugar in a skillet over medium heat. When the sugar starts to melt, add the butter and stir to blend with a whisk or wooden spoon. ✪ When the mixture becomes liquid and very hot, add the bananas all at once. ✪ Stir to coat the bananas with the syrup. Remove from heat and let cool. ✪ Serve the bananas at once or store them the refrigerator for up to 2 days. Stir again before serving.

Cowboy Coffee

★ ★ ★ ★ ★ ★ ★ ★ ★ ★ ★ ★ ★ ★ ★ ★ ★ ★ ★ ★

Coffee goes great with pie, but of course, to a cowboy, coffee goes great with anything. Old-time cowboys drank strong black coffee first thing in the morning; before, during, after, and between meals; and just before bed at night. Cowboy coffee was never filtered. The grounds were boiled in the pot. The old chuck-wagon cooks used to say that, to test coffee, you drop a horseshoe in the pot. If the horseshoe floats, the coffee's strong enough.

We use a dark-roasted, whole-bean blend called CF Ranch Cowboy Coffee at the Reata, and we sell it by the pound to our customers. To order some, call (800) 409-7878.

Biscuit Pudding with Southern Comfort Cream

YIELD: 9 SERVINGS

Biscuits should always be served hot out of the oven. Save your leftover biscuits in a plastic bag until you have enough to make this biscuit pudding. This will taste best if you used the optional pecans in those biscuits.

6 cups roughly crumbled Buttermilk
  Pecan Biscuits (page 97)

3 eggs

1 (14-ounce) can sweetened condensed milk

1 cup heavy cream

$^1/_2$ teaspoon pure vanilla extract

3 tablespoons unsalted butter, melted

1 teaspoon freshly squeezed lemon juice

1 teaspoon kosher salt

2 cups Southern Comfort Cream
  (recipe follows)

✪ Preheat the oven to 300°. ✪ Butter an 8 by 8-inch pan and set it aside. ✪ In a large mixing bowl, beat the eggs. ✪ Add the milk and cream and whisk to blend. ✪ Add the remaining ingredients, except the Southern Comfort Cream. ✪ Toss everything together and pour into the prepared pan. ✪ Bake for 1 hour. A knife inserted near the middle will come out moist but clean when pudding is cooked. ✪ Serve warm with the Southern Comfort Cream.

Variation

Spotted Pup: toss $1^1/_2$ cups of raisins, Dried Fruit Mixture (page 201), or chocolate chips in with the biscuits and proceed as directed.

Southern Comfort Cream

YIELD: 2 CUPS

This whiskey cream sauce tastes great on any kind of bread pudding.

$^1/_2$ **cup unsalted butter**
$^1/_2$ **cup sugar**
1 cup heavy cream
$^1/_3$ **cup Southern Comfort**

✪ Melt the butter over medium heat in a saucepan. ✪ Slowly add the sugar to the butter, stirring with a wooden spoon. ✪ Cook the mixture for approximately 3 minutes, or until the sugar dissolves. The mixture will be opaque, not clear. ✪ Add the cream, stirring constantly, and cook to bring the temperature to 180°. Use a candy thermometer to check the temperature, remembering not to touch the bottom of the pan. ✪ Let the mixture simmer for 5 minutes. ✪ Remove the pan from the heat and stir in the Southern Comfort. ✪ Serve the sauce warm with the Biscuit Pudding, or cool it for future use. ✪ Cool the mixture quickly by inserting the pan into an ice bath. ✪ When cool, store it in the refrigerator.

Buñuelos

YIELD: 9 PASTRIES

These flaky pastries are traditionally served in Mexico with hot chocolate on Christmas morning. The Raspberry Cointreau Sauce turns them into a nice light dessert.

4 cups flour
1 teaspoon kosher salt
2 teaspoons baking powder
$1/_4$ cup solid vegetable shortening
$1/_2$ to 1 cup warm water
$1/_2$ cup sugar
3 tablespoons ground cinnamon
10 cups peanut oil
$2^1/_2$ cups Raspberry Cointreau Sauce
   (recipe follows)

✪ Combine the flour, salt, baking powder, and shortening in a mixer fitted with a paddle attachment. ✪ Mix on low speed until well blended. ✪ With the mixer running, slowly add the water, waiting until the water is absorbed before continuing. The water should bind the flour mixture and make a soft dough that is not sticky. The amount of water will vary each time. Let the dough rest for 15 minutes. ✪ Remove the dough from the bowl and knead lightly. Portion the dough into 3-ounce balls (you should have 9 pieces, if you don't have a scale). ✪ Roll each ball into a thin circle the size of a tortilla, about 6 to 8 inches across. ✪ Stack each round between sheets of wax paper. Set these aside until cooking time. ✪ Combine the sugar and cinnamon in a small bowl and set aside.

✪ Heat the oil in a deep, heavy pan to 350°, or until a piece of dough sizzles. ✪ Use a thermometer to help maintain a constant temperature. ✪ When the correct temperature is reached, slide 1 or 2 rounds into the hot oil. ✪ Cook the rounds for 2 to 3 minutes, turning once, until they are golden brown and slightly puffed. ✪ Remove the Buñuelos and drain them on a pan lined with paper towels. ✪ Repeat until all the dough is cooked. ✪ Sprinkle the Buñuelos with the cinnamon-sugar mixture while still warm and serve with Raspberry Cointreau Sauce.

Buñuelos

Raspberry Cointreau Sauce

YIELD: ABOUT $1^1/_2$ CUPS

You can make this sauce with fresh raspberries or any other kind of fresh berries you have on hand, but frozen raspberries make things simple.

12 ounces frozen raspberries
3 tablespoons sugar
4 tablespoons Cointreau
4 tablespoons water

✪ Place the raspberries, sugar, Cointreau, and water in a saucepan and bring them to a boil. ✪ Reduce the heat and simmer for 5 minutes, or until the berries are soft. ✪ Transfer the mixture to a blender and purée. ✪ Pass the mixture through a fine strainer, such as a chinois, pressing with the back of a spoon to extract all of the liquid. ✪ Discard the seeds. ✪ Serve this sauce with Buñuelos, or store it in a covered container in the refrigerator for another use.

Cajeta Pound Cake

YIELD: 1 BUNDT CAKE, ABOUT 12 SERVINGS

This simple pound cake is a great way to feature the flavor of cajeta. It makes a great dessert, but I also love it for breakfast with some good strong coffee.

1¹/₂ cups unsalted butter, softened

3 cups sugar

8 eggs

4 cups sifted flour

2 teaspoons baking powder

1 teaspoon kosher salt

2 cups Cajeta Sauce (page 188)

✪ Preheat the oven to 350°. ✪ Grease the inside of a Bundt pan. ✪ Dust lightly with flour, shake out excess, and set aside. ✪ Cream the butter and sugar in a mixer fitted with a paddle attachment until the mixture is light in color and texture. ✪ Add the eggs one at a time, blending well after each addition. ✪ Stop and scrape the bowl with a spatula as needed. Beat the mixture until it is light in color, about 3 minutes. ✪ Sift the flour, baking powder, and salt together and then add to the creamed mixture, blending at low speed. ✪ Increase the speed and beat the mixture for 2 minutes. ✪ Fold in the *cajeta* sauce with the mixer running at the lowest speed. ✪ Pour batter into the prepared pan. ✪ Bake the cake for 1 hour and 15 minutes. ✪ Begin to test cake after 1 hour, with a toothpick. An inserted toothpick will come out clean when the cake is done. ✪ Remove the cake from the oven and let it cool. ✪ Turn the cake out onto a serving plate. The cake may be chilled in the refrigerator.

Cajeta Pound Cake

Apple Crisp with Cajeta

Apple Crisp with Cajeta

YIELD: 8 SERVINGS

Cobblers, crisps, and buckles were always the most common desserts in cowboy cooking. The cajeta topping gives this apple crisp an unexpected but delicious twist.

8 Granny Smith apples, peeled and cored
1 cup heavy cream
$1/_2$ cup sugar
$1/_4$ cup flour
1 tablespoon ground cinnamon
1 tablespoon freshly squeezed lemon juice
$1/_2$ teaspoon kosher salt

TOPPING
$1^1/_2$ cups flour
1 cup packed light brown sugar
2 teaspoons ground cinnamon
$1/_4$ teaspoon kosher salt
12 tablespoons cold, unsalted butter
Cajeta Sauce (page 188)

✪ Butter a 9 by 13-inch pan. ✪ Slice the apples into thin wedges. ✪ Toss the apple slices in a large bowl with the cream, sugar, flour, cinnamon, lemon juice, and salt. ✪ Layer the apples into the prepared pan. Preheat oven to 350°.

✪ To make the topping: Mix the flour, brown sugar, cinnamon, and salt in a bowl. ✪ Cut the cold butter into small pieces and blend it with the dry mixture, using a fork or your hands. ✪ The mixture should not be overworked. It will look crumbly. ✪ Spread the topping over the apples. ✪ Bake for 45 minutes to 1 hour, or until the apples are soft and mixture is bubbling. ✪ Serve warm with *Cajeta Sauce* drizzled on top.

Cajeta Sauce (Caramel Sauce)

YIELD: APPROXIMATELY 4 CUPS

Cajeta is goat's milk caramel, and it's used in some of the most delicious desserts in Mexico. You can buy a bottle of cajeta sauce in a Mexican grocery store, or you can make it from fresh goat's milk the way we do at Reata.

4 cups sugar

1 cup water

$^1/_4$ cup unsalted butter

1 to 2 cups heavy cream or fresh goat's milk

✪ Combine the sugar and water in a large, wide, heavy saucepan and bring it to a boil. ✪ Use a pan in which you can see the color of the sugar as it cooks. Stir as needed to dissolve sugar. Do not stir again once the mixture begins to simmer. ✪ Continue a steady boil to reduce the mixture and bring it to a light brown color. This may take 20 to 30 minutes. When the light brown color is reached, watch carefully as it changes to golden brown. It should be fairly thick. ✪ At this moment, remove it from the heat and slowly stir the butter into the sugar syrup. ✪ Blend in enough cream to make the consistency fairly thick, yet still golden brown in color.

✪ As sauce cools, it becomes thicker. ✪ Serve *cajeta* warm. ✪ Store any extra in the refrigerator.

Cowboy Brownies

YIELD: 15 SERVINGS

For exceptional brownies, use a great milk chocolate like Lindt. I like to eat these brownies while they're still warm and gooey, with a big scoop of vanilla ice cream on top.

4 $1/_2$ cups (about 1$3/_4$ pounds) bittersweet
  chocolate chunks
1 cup unsalted butter, cut into pieces
8 eggs
3 cups sugar
1$1/_2$ cups flour
$1/_2$ cup cocoa powder
4 teaspoons pure vanilla extract
3 cups chopped pecans
1 cup (about 6 ounces) milk chocolate chunks
Vanilla ice cream (optional)

✪ Preheat the oven to 325°. ✪ Butter a 13 by 9 by 2-inch baking pan and set it aside.

✪ Combine 3 cups (about 1 pound) of the bittersweet chocolate with the butter and melt it in a bowl in the microwave or in a saucepan over low heat on the stove. When the butter and chocolate are melted, set aside.

✪ In a mixer, using the paddle attachment, beat the eggs for 3 minutes on medium speed. ✪ Add the sugar and continue to beat until the mixture is light in color and texture. ✪ Add the melted chocolate and combine well. Mix the flour and cocoa together and add them to the chocolate mixture, along with the vanilla. ✪ Fold the nuts, the remaining 1$1/_2$ cups bittersweet chocolate chunks, and the milk chocolate chunks into the mixture by hand or with a mixer on low speed. ✪ Spread the mixture into the prepared pan using a spatula. ✪ Place this pan in a larger pan and pour boiling water halfway up the sides of the larger pan to create a hot water bath. ✪ Place the pans in the oven and bake the mixture for 40 to 45 minutes. ✪ Remove the pans from the oven and remove brownies from the water bath to allow them to cool. ✪ Serve slightly warm, with ice cream if desired.

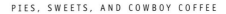

Dessert Tostadas with Ice Cream, Strawberries, and White Chocolate

Dessert Tostadas with Ice Cream, Strawberries, and White Chocolate

YIELD: 5 SERVINGS

These dessert tostadas look just like regular tostadas!

FOR TOSTADA SHELLS:

$1/_3$ cup packed brown sugar

$1/_4$ cup unsalted butter

$1^1/_2$ tablespoons light corn syrup

$1/_8$ teaspoon pure vanilla extract

$3/_4$ cup flour

TO FINISH TOSTADAS

1 pint vanilla ice cream

$1^1/_4$ cups diced fresh strawberries

$1^1/_4$ cups Caramelized Bananas
(page 179)

$1/_4$ cup julienned mint leaves

$1/_3$ cup grated white chocolate
(about $1^1/_2$ ounces)

✪ To prepare the tostada shells, heat the sugar, butter, corn syrup, and vanilla in a heavy saucepan. ✪ Bring to a boil and stir the mixture over medium heat until the butter melts and the sugar dissolves. ✪ Remove mixture from the heat and whisk in the flour until batter is very thick and a creamy, caramel color. There should be no flour showing. ✪ Preheat oven to 400°. Prepare two 17 by 12-inch pans by lining with parchment paper. ✪ Secure paper to the pan with dabs of butter around the edges. (This keeps the paper in place during the spreading and cooking process.) ✪ Divide the batter between the two pans and spread each portion in an even, solid, thin layer using a plastic pastry scraper or a spatula. The batter will not reach the edges and it will be almost transparent. ✪ Place the pans into the oven and bake about 5 minutes, or until the mixture is golden brown and begins to look bubbly. The thickness of the batter will determine the exact cooking time. ✪ Remove pans from the oven and immediately cut 3-inch rounds with a biscuit cutter, cutting as close as possible to each other. You should get about 10 rounds. ✪ Leave them in place to cool and become brittle. ✪ Remove when hard and set aside until serving time in an airtight container.

✪ Place 2 tostadas on each plate. ✪ Center a small scoop of ice cream on each tostada, and top each serving with $1/_4$ cup each of the strawberries and Caramelized Bananas. Sprinkle with a bit of mint and 1 tablespoon white chocolate per serving. ✪ Serve at once.

10

Chuck Box Secrets

DURING SPRING ROUNDUP, cowboys on horseback still roam over hundreds of thousands of acres of the Trans-Pecos. The cowboys camp outside for the month or so it takes them to round up all the cattle on each ranch. The cooking is done from a motorized version of the old-fashioned chuck wagon—a pickup truck with a chuck box mounted on the back.

A chuck box is sort of a portable pantry, a big wooden cabinet with lots of drawers and compartments to hold all the cooking equipment and dry ingredients. To cut down on cooking time and make the most of the chuck box's storage space, modern cowboy cooks usually grind their chile powders, blend up their spice mixes, and cook up their barbecue sauces in advance. And they always have lots of little jars of mysterious stuff stashed away, which they call their secret ingredients.

Like most restaurants, we do the same sort of prep work at Reata. If you're going to use the same spice mix or sauce in lots of different recipes, you might as well make up a big batch and keep plenty on hand. It's a lot faster and easier to cook good food if you already have top-notch ingredients ready to go.

The biggest problem in home cooking is that nobody has the time to do a lot of prep work. Good home cooks know that fresh ground chiles and commercial chile powder are as different as night and day, that roasted shallots have a mellower flavor than minced fresh shallots, and that cracked pepper has a texture that even coarsely ground fresh pepper can't match. But even for the best home cooks, the extra steps are sometimes ridiculous. Taking a half hour to roast shallots when you're just trying to make a cup of salad dressing or grinding fresh whole chiles when all you need is a sprinkle is a waste of time in anybody's book.

But most of these things are a cinch if you have a little advance notice. It's pretty easy to shove some shallots in the oven when you've got something else roasting or to throw some tomatoes on the smoker after the meat's done. And grinding up an extra dried pepper or two is no big deal when you're already making chili. So keep the recipes in this chapter in mind while you're cooking other dishes. You'll be amazed what a difference it makes when you have these secret ingredients in your chuck box.

Handling Chile Peppers

It's wise to wear rubber gloves when handling any kind of chile pepper. Get a little juice from the cut-up pepper on your face or in your eyes and you can count on 10 minutes of sheer agony. If you don't have rubber gloves, use a paper towel or a piece of plastic wrap to hold the pepper while you cut it. Clean your hands, the knife, and the cutting board immediately with hot soapy water.

Roasted Peppers (Poblanos and Green Chiles)

Lightly oil the surface of the peppers. Roast the peppers over a flame or under a broiler until they are charred on all sides. Set them aside in a plastic bag for 10 minutes to allow the steam to loosen the skin from the pepper. Peel off the charred skin and discard it. Slit one side of the pepper down the middle, remove and discard the seeds, and set the peppers aside until serving time. Peeled, roasted peppers can be stored in the refrigerator for 2 or 3 days or for up to 3 months in a resealable plastic bag in the freezer.

Peppers

Pasilla Powder

YIELD: 1 CUP

You won't believe what a difference it makes to use your own fresh ground peppers instead of commercial chile powder. Try it. It's really easy. Just be sure to clean out the coffee grinder real good when you're done.

5 pasilla chiles

✪ Prepare the pasilla chiles by removing the stem and seeds. ✪ Toast the peppers in a skillet over medium heat for 5 minutes, turning them frequently until they are dry and crisp, but not burned. ✪ Purée the peppers in a coffee grinder until they become a fine powder.

Variations

Ancho Powder: Use 5 ancho peppers instead of the pasillas and proceed as directed.

Guajillo Powder: Use 5 *guajillo* peppers instead of the pasillas and proceed as directed.

Red Chile Paste

YIELD: 4 $^{1}/_{2}$ TO 5 CUPS

The New Mexican dried chiles give this purée its bright red color and the anchos give it a rich raisiny flavor. You can vary the dried chiles if you want to make different kinds of chile pastes.

4 ancho chiles

4 New Mexican dried chiles or Mexican guajillos

3 cups chicken stock

$^{1}/_{2}$ white onion, diced

3 cloves garlic, minced

✪ Slit each chile with a sharp knife and remove the seeds and stem. ✪ Place the peppers in a large saucepan and cover them with the chicken stock. ✪ Add the onion and garlic. ✪ Bring the stock to a boil over high heat, reduce heat, and allow to simmer for about 15 minutes, or until the peppers have absorbed some liquid and have become soft. ✪ Pour the pepper mixture and cooking liquid into a blender. ✪ Blend on low speed, increasing to high speed as the purée combines.

Variation

Chipotle Red Chile Paste: For a hotter and smokier flavor, add 1 or more canned chipotles to the blender just before processing.

Roasted Garlic

You can roast some garlic while you've got a chicken or a pork roast in the oven. But don't try roasting garlic in the same oven with a pie or a batch of cookies. It's very aromatic, and it'll make your dessert taste weird.

3 whole heads garlic
3 teaspoons olive oil
1 sprig thyme, stems removed

✪ Preheat the oven to 350°. ✪ Peel away any excess outer skin from the garlic and make a thin cut off the top to expose the cloves. ✪ Set the garlic in a small baking dish or on a piece of foil. ✪ Drizzle the top with oil and sprinkle it with thyme. ✪ Cover or wrap the garlic tightly in foil and bake it for 45 minutes to 1 hour, or until the garlic is soft and aromatic. ✪ Let it cool slightly. ✪ Gently squeeze the cloves out of their peeling and mash them with a fork or purée them in a food processor. ✪ Store in the refrigerator until ready for use.

Roasted Shallots

I love the flavor of roasted shallots in salad dressings and sauces. They keep for a week or so in the fridge.

$1/_2$ pound shallots (about 6 large shallots)
3 teaspoons olive oil

✪ Preheat the oven to 350°. ✪ Peel the shallots and cut them into quarters if they are large. ✪ Lightly coat each piece of shallot with oil, place them on a pan covered with foil, and roast them for 15 minutes, or until they are soft and beginning to brown. ✪ Remove the shallots and let them cool. ✪ Gently squeeze the cloves out of their peeling and mash them with a fork or purée them in a food processor. ✪ Store the shallots in the refrigerator until ready for use.

Cracked Pepper

Cracked pepper is very different from freshly ground pepper. The aroma and flavor of the peppercorn comes through in every bite.

To make cracked pepper, you need to crush each peppercorn into no more than eight or ten pieces. You can put whole peppercorns in a large frying pan and use a smaller frying pan to crush them, but you really need to bear down hard and this takes a lot of strength.

The easiest cracking method is to put the peppercorns in a food processor and pulse it once or twice. This method takes patience and usually requires several batches. You have to sort through the cracked peppercorns, remove the remaining whole peppercorns and repeat the process.

The simplest way to keep cracked peppercorns in your chuck box is to buy a bottle of whole black peppercorns, crack them all, and return them to the same bottle for storage.

Smoked Tomatoes

We use smoked tomatoes in our guacamole, but smoked tomatoes are also the secret of truly great salsas.

Place tomatoes in a stove-top smoker for 7 minutes, or on an outdoor smoker for $1/_2$ hour. Smoking times will vary with the season. Roma tomatoes tend to take longer. Tender summer tomatoes will not take long at all. The result you are looking for is a flavorful, firm tomato, not a cooked tomato.

Reata Grill Blend

ÝIELD: ABOUT 1 CUP

Our homemade steak seasoning mix is addictive—put some in a jar in your pantry and you'll find yourself using it on everything.

4 tablespoons kosher salt

3 tablespoons Pasilla Powder (page 196)

2 tablespoons dried granulated garlic

2 tablespoons sugar

2 tablespoons ground cumin

2 tablespoons coarsely ground black pepper

1 tablespoon ground thyme

✪ Combine all of the ingredients in a small bowl, blending well to evenly distribute the spices. Be sure to break up any chunks that appear. ✪ Store the blend in an airtight container. Shake or stir it again before each use.

Molasses Rub

YIELD: 1 CUP

This is an easy glaze for a roasted chicken or a baked ham.

1 cup packed light brown sugar

2 tablespoons molasses

$1^1/_2$ teaspoons kosher salt

2 teaspoons paprika

$1^1/_2$ teaspoons freshly ground pepper

2 teaspoons dried thyme leaves

1 teaspoon garlic powder

✪ Combine the ingredients in the bowl of a food processor and process until the mixture is well blended. ✪ Remove the rub and use it as needed, or store it in an airtight container.

Spicy Pecans

YIELD: 4 CUPS

Coated pecans are great in salads, as a snack with cheese, or all by themselves with a cold beer.

4 cups (about 1 pound) pecan halves
6 tablespoons unsalted butter, melted
4 teaspoons Pasilla Powder (page 196)
$^1/_2$ cup packed brown sugar

✪ Preheat oven to 350°. ✪ In a large bowl, toss the pecans and butter until all surfaces are coated. ✪ Sprinkle the chile powder over the nuts and again combine well. ✪ Add the sugar and toss using your hands to keep the sugar from lumping. ✪ Dump the entire mixture onto a sheet pan, scraping the residue in the bowl on top of the nuts. ✪ Bake the nuts in the oven for 20 minutes, or until the coating on the nuts begins to brown and the sugar melts. The coating at this point will not be crunchy, but as the nuts cool, the coating will harden. ✪ Store nuts in an airtight container until needed.

Dried Fruit Mixture

YIELD: 2 CUPS

$^1/_2$ cup dried papayas, cut into $^1/_4$-inch dice
$^1/_2$ cup dried pineapples, cut into $^1/_4$-inch dice
$^1/_2$ cup raisins
$^1/_2$ cup dried cranberries.

✪ Combine all ingredients and store in an airtight container.

Cook's Butters

Butter mixed with herbs or chiles is one of my favorite steak toppings. You soften the butter, mix in the seasonings, and then freeze the butter into a cylinder and slice it. It's easy to do and it adds a nice touch of color and flavor to simple grilled meats. Cook's butters are also great on sourdough biscuits and breads. Here's a couple of flavors to choose from.

Cilantro Butter

YIELD: 8 1-OUNCE PORTIONS

2 cups loosely packed cilantro leaves
1 cup unsalted butter, softened
Kosher salt to taste

✪ Finely chop the cilantro leaves or place them in the container of a food processor and process. The processor method will give a greener color to the finished butter. ✪ Place the cilantro, butter, and salt in a mixer fitted with a paddle attachment and beat at medium speed until the butter is light and fluffy. ✪ Remove the butter from the bowl, place on a length of parchment paper or foil, and roll into a $1^1/_2$-inch-wide cylinder, squeezing gently to remove any air pockets. ✪ Freeze the butter until ready for use. Just before serving time, thaw the butter for 10 minutes. ✪ Then cut it into thin disks. ✪ Serve it cold. The butter will keep in the freezer for up to 3 months.

Variations

Roasted Garlic Butter: Blend 2 tablespoons Roasted Garlic (page 198) purée with the butter, until the butter is light and fluffy. Season it with salt and pepper to taste. Proceed as directed above.

Chile Butter: Measure 5 teaspoons of freshly ground pasilla, ancho, or *guajillo* powder and blend it with the butter until light and fluffy. Season the butter with salt and pepper to taste. Proceed as directed above.

Chipotle BBQ Sauce

YIELD: ABOUT 4 CUPS

I hate to give out this recipe. We Texans have always kept this barbecue sauce a secret from those guys up in Kansas City.

1 tablespoon oil

2 cups diced yellow onion

7 cloves garlic, minced

1 cup ketchup

1 cup Chipotle Red Chile Paste (page 197)

$^1/_2$ cup Worcestershire sauce

$^1/_2$ cup strong coffee

$^1/_3$ cup packed brown sugar

$^1/_4$ cup cider vinegar

$^1/_4$ cup freshly squeezed lemon juice

$1^1/_2$ tablespoons Dijon mustard

2 teaspoons kosher salt

✪ In a large, heavy saucepan, heat the oil over medium heat and add the onion and garlic. ✪ Sauté until they begin to wilt. ✪ Add the ketchup and chile paste and sauté for 4 minutes. ✪ Add all of the remaining ingredients, stir, and let them simmer for 30 to 40 minutes. As the sauce thickens, stir more often so it does not scorch. ✪ Remove the sauce from the heat and allow it to cool. ✪ Place the sauce in a blender and purée it. ✪ Store it in the refrigerator.

Chipotle BBQ Sauce

Bibliography

Andrews, Jean. *Peppers: The Domesticated Capsicums*, second edition. Austin: University of Texas Press, 1995.

Barrios, Virginia B. *A Guide to Tequila, Mezcal and Pulque*. Claremont, Calif.: Ocelot Press, 1971.

Bayless, Rick. *Authentic Mexican*. New York: Morrow, 1987.

Dearden, Patrick. *A Cowboy of the Pecos*. Plano, Texas: Republic of Texas Press, 1997.

Dobie, J. Frank. *A Vaquero of the Brush Country*. Temecula, Calif.: Reprint services, 1993 (originally published by Southwest Press, 1929).

Ferber, Edna. *Giant*. Cutchogue, N.Y.: Buccaneer Books, 1991.

Luchetti, Cathy. *Home on the Range: A Culinary History of the American West*. New York: Villard, 1993.

Price, Byron B. *National Cowboy Hall of Fame Chuck Wagon Cookbook*. New York: Hearst Books, 1995.

Stillwell, Hallie Crawford. *I'll Gather My Geese*. College Station: Texas A&M University Press, 1995.

Thorne, John. *Serious Pig*. New York: North Point Press, 1996.

Tolbert, Frank X. *A Bowl of Red*. New York: Doubleday, 1967 (out of print).

Index